Positive feelings bring us happiness

Book content:

I0415435

Prologue

Feelings are very important in our lives and can be positive and negative. Positive feelings make our live more pleasant and happy, they can form, develop and maintain.

Forming, developing and maintaining them can prevent forming negative feelings. It is necessary to form and maintain positive feelings day by day, as long as we live and we must prevent forming negative feelings.

The ideas in books about feelings and AGC thoughts help us a lot to form, develop and maintain positive feelings and prevent forming negative feelings.

The ideas in this book and other are necessary day by day, as long as we live, to succeed in life and accomplish our objectives.

Only a positive thinking help us in life, marriage, love and other activities, to rich our personal objectives, solve and prevent new problems.

Ideas in this book help us a lot. It help us to form and develop our positive thinking, to understand how to prevent major problems and solve problems already appeared.

The money investment in this book of mine and the others that follow it is worth it, and it is almost nothing comparing to the positive effects that this book can have in your life.

These books contain lots of positive, optimist, creative, dinamic ideas, that push you to action, to thinking, things that are necesary your daily life and to accomplish your personal objectives.

Some of the ideas we might all know but when we need them mostly (in griefs, failures, when we want to have a solution to our problems), we don't remember them to help us when we need.

Reading and analizing the ideas in this book and aplying them, we'll find solutions and ideas that will help us find:
I. To discover:
1. defects
2. qualities
3. capabilities
4. qualifications
5. some opportunities to succeed in life
6. feelings
7. what we do to be loved
8. how to love
9. how to realize and maintain a true mutual love
10. how to realize and maintain a happy marriage

11. mistakes, errors, wrong ideas
12. etc.

II. To prevent some:
1. mistakes
2. divorces
3. suspect
4. griefs
5. conflicts
6. accidents
7. failures
8. bankruptcy
9. etc.

III. To become more:
1. happy
2. loved
3. honored,
4. appreciated,
5. wanted,
6. optimistic,
7. good,
8. unselfish,
9. emotional,
10. altruists
11. stronger
12. efficient
13. organized
14. planners
15. active

16. honest
17. human
18. popular
19. famous
20. flexible
21. adaptable
22. understanding
23. prompt
24. etc

IV.   To get out of a state of:
1. despair
2. pessimism
3. passiveness
4. inactivity
5. inefficiency
6. inflexibility
7. crisis
8. inadaptability
9. etc.

V.   To participate more actively to:
1. social life
2. political life
3. nonprofit organizations activities
4. etc

VI.   To participate more actively and efficiently in achieving true love and a happy marriage

VII.   To find more likely situations conducive to achieving and

maintaining a happy marriage life
VIII. To change our life for the better and to make it more beautiful
IX. To multiply and increase the chances to find your life partner
X. To raise and educate our children better so we can take better care of them
XI. Find more and bigger chances to meet favorable situations to accomplish and maintain a happy marriage for life.
XII. Change our life in good and make it better.
XIII. To multiply and increase the chances to find your life partner
XIV. To raise and educate our children better so we can take better care of them

I write and gather these thoughts, ideas in books, internet and other publications because these are useful to us every day and it is necessary to apply them to accomplish what we want, a better and beautiful life and prosperous.

These thoughts reflect a small part of what is good in reality and human relationships.

I wait to hear from you good news, good deeds that you have done influenced from what you have read from these books to make your life more beautiful, prosperous, happier and to be a positive example for others.

Each of us can become positive examples for others around us, participating to the creation of a better, prosperous and happier human society.

I'd be happy if one or more ideas read from these books helped you in a way or another and made you happier and prosperous.

I'm waiting to hear from you, your ideas and opinions, your joys and griefes and your suggestions for new book subjects and i also appeal to your participation of promoting on the internet and mass media of the ideas and the books i've written.

Dear readers I wish you all health, happiness and achievement of all your wishes.

I invite you to e-mail me at my email address: agcornel@gmail.com

Best regards and respect:

Ardelean Gheorghe Cornel
981 Principal Street
Macea, county Arad
Zip Code 371210
Romania
Tel # (40)-0788-725-204
(40)-0788-725-913

Abandon

1. We should never abandon our realistic goals.

2. Society has no right to abandon its people who need protection without protection, without shelter, living on the streets, canals, etc.. without a minimum of shelter and food for a normal living.

Abuse

3. Societies make "n" abuses against the unprotected, by not protecting them.

4. The society makes "n" abuses against the unprotected, by not protecting them.

5. A judge makes a lesser mistake if he gives a smaller sentence than to abuse and be wrong so as to give an illegally bigger punishment.

6. Women are mostly abused in family violence.

7. Not respecting the right to nondiscrimination of people by the state is a great abuse.

8. Abuse must be discouraged by the law.

9. Many times abuse causes many negative effects.

10. Most abuses can be prevented with the help of an effective law.

11. Constructive thinking makes us have zero tolerance towards abuse.

12. All types of abuse in society can and must be prevented in time.

13. Any abuse may cause another or other abuse.

14. The law must prevent any possible abuse.

15. Abuse must be prevented by law.

Accept

16. My meditations push us, give us impulses to achieve a better world. Read, analyze them and apply those you accept. Good luck.

17. Thought my help you can prevent many mistakes. Read, analyze them and apply those you accept. Good luck!

18. Love for the vast majority of women is particularly important. Given this fact in having a relationship of true love, unfortunately, many facts are unacceptable.

19. Life without true love for many young people is unacceptable.

20. My meditations help us achieve and maintain a happy marriage. Read, analyze and apply those that you accept. Good luck.

21. Some people call crazy all those who have ideas that they do not accept.

22. Lack of common sense is an unacceptable defect of any man.

23. Any act of family aggression, made by a family member against another member of the family can not be reasoned and legally bound to be accepted under any circumstances.

24. The one who is superficial in what he does is not accepted and employed by many employers.

25. Rudeness is an unacceptable defect.

26. Although rudeness is unacceptable in the XXI century, it is still too widespread.

27. Constructive thinking does not accept the non-abiding of human rights.

28. Arrogance between spouses is unacceptable.

29. Each woman has the need to feel accepted.

30. Although many scientific researches have found that smoking damages very much our

health, even that of those who are non-smokers, all countries accept the legal industry and related trade of cigarettes, which cause tens and hundreds of millions of illnesses and deaths. The situation is incredible, but unfortunately, it exists in all of the world's states. Why do we even tolerate such incredibly damageable activities for billions of people, with incalculable negative effects?

31.   He who brutal is not accepted by most people.

32.   There are people who do not accept jokes.

Accomplish

33.   Our successes increase our strength, our confidence in our own forces and the accomplishment of other successes.

34.   By living our lives at random, happiness too can only be accomplished randomly.

35.   The more positive and humane deeds we accomplish, the more we increase our chances of being happy.

36.   In life it is necessary to enjoy every achievement, any accomplishments no matter how small if we want and act and to achieve more and greater successes.

37. There are circumstances in which, for certain news, accomplishments, etc. we can feel happy, but we can not be fully happy, for some reason, for example, because someone close to us has died.

38. Optimistic people have achieved the great accomplishments of mankind.

39. Ideas that can change our lives for the better can be found in books, on the Internet, in periodicals and newspapers, from people who have great accomplishments, those with so much experience.

40. The fact that we do not have certain assets, accomplishments, etc. during certain periods of our life must not fret, consume, frustrate, make us unhappy, but it is necessary to enjoy what we have, what we have achieved, the projects that we have to achieve, the qualities, the skills that we have, etc.

41. In life we may each receive more or less unjust blows. No unjust blow should consume us, because if we consume ourselves we do not solve anything but instead we harm us and sometimes even very much and we also complicate some problems that we have.

42. First of all when we receive an unjust blow, we should focus on finding solutions, actions

to help us minimize the negative effects of the blow, unless we can reduce them to zero.

43. Secondly, it is necessary to identify the causes and factors that led us to receiving them unjustly.

44. Thirdly, it is necessary to remove the causes that led us to receiving them unjustly, so that we shall not receive them again or several times again.

45. In the fourth line is necessary to take all necessary measures to prevent the causes that led us to reciving the X blow unjustly.

46. Fifthly it is necessary to seek to identify whether there are other causes that might lead us to receive further blows unjustly.

47. Sixthly it is necessary to discover other potential causes that could cause us to receive more unfair blows by taking the necessary measures: 1) to eliminate these causes, 2) where we can not prevent these causes it is necessary to take the necessary measures not to receive them unjustly, 3) if we receive them, to make the blow have as little negative effects as possible over us.

48. In the seventh line it is necessary that our new situation caused by the unfair blow is used efficiently for us. It is possible that what

we accomplish after the new situation created by the unjustly received blow is much larger and beneficial to us than the achievements that we had done if we had not received the blow unjustly.

49. In life, we can continuously increase our credibility before people. This is accomplished when our actions are positive and visible and we continuously have positive visible actions.

50. The desire to succeed in life can be accomplished with the help of efficient co operations.

51. Accomplishing global thinking is also accelerated by the exchange of information.

52. Accomplishing exchanges of information helps achieve more and greater successes.

53. A proper motivation of people leads to accomplishing more and greater successes.

54. The calculated man manages to accomplish smaller or greater successes.

55. Those who have the same interests may unite and accomplished them.

56. Accomplishing exchanges of information helps us prevent many failures.

57. A man with practical values manages to accomplish efficient co operations.

58. Those who passionately live their life will mostly succeed in achieving many accomplishments.

59. A full compatibility of training with the objectives is achieved also through efficient accomplishments of social reality.

60. A man with tactical values accomplishes himself in life.

61. Accomplishing exchanges of information helps us a lot to achieve perfection.

62. Those who have high objectives in life need to achieve more efficient co operations in order to accomplish their high objectives.

63. The sense of achievement and quality in everything we do increases our ability to accomplish more outstanding performances.

64. People who can prevent possible mistakes accomplish a happy marriage.

65. Not achieving objectives can be accomplished through using positive ideas.

66. The desire to make others happy can be accomplished through the contribution of the formation, development, maintenance and usage of positive thinking.

67. A great desire to achieve successes helps us accomplish effective co operations.

68. The desire to succeed in life increases our chances of accomplishing our personal goals.

69. A realistic man in interpersonal relations has greater chances to accomplish effective co operations.

70. Love is not accomplished by itself but by us.

71. We can contribute to the achievement of our greatest accomplishments also through the contribution of the formation, development, maintenance and usage of charitable behavior.

72. A great capacity of accomplishing strategies of applying thinking on a big scale helps us become optimistic.

73. We can contribute to the achievement of our greatest accomplishments also through the contribution of the formation, development, maintenance and usage of convincing behavior.

74. A great capacity of accomplishing strategies of applying thinking on a big scale helps us become happy.

75. The ability to accomplish personal objectives helps us achieve more records.

76. The passion of accomplishing successes helps us achieve more favorable situations.

77. The desire to accomplish records helps us achieve more efficient co operations.

78. The power used to accomplish positive deeds helps us achieve more records.

79. The passion of accomplishing successes helps us achieve more true friendships.

80. The ability to accomplish personal objectives helps us achieve more favorable chances.

Achieve

81. When we are depressed it is necessary to get in contact with optimistic people and to do things which bring us success, achievements and hopes.

82. Most of us do not have as a permanent objective the achievement of a good life and we are not even seriously concerned to reach it. So how can we have a beautiful life?

83. Life can be more beautiful if we set as a priority the objective of achieving a good life

and if we continuously work to achieve this objective.

84. Perseverance often helps us achieve our objectives.

85. We can achieve our objectives much easier if we apply the ideas in these books, etc..

86. In life, we can achieve even more good deeds if we persevere in carrying out many good deeds.

87. We can act to achieve several prioritary objectives at the same time.

88. It is necessary to give prioritary objectives the time necessary to be achieved in due time.

89. Proper planning of our actions increases our chances to achieve successes.

90. Perseverance is one of those weapons that achieve successes.

91. Long term thinking has led to the achievement of many very high successes.

92. We can achieve objectives only if they are achievable.

93. Practical ideas most often lead us to the achievement of bigger or smaller successes.

94. Most of us could become happy if we set as a goal to become happy and if we act to achieve it.

95. Each of us has the chance to assert oneself in real life. It is important to discover the chances and to achieve the goal.

96. In many situations patience helps us to achieve great successes.

97. By acting continuously and effectively to achieve positive goals we will surely achieve them.

98. Through solidarity we can achieve much more performances.

99. Through unity we can achieve much more performances.

100. Those who will consider wise advice, will have much greater opportunities to achieve success.

101. By good co-living, we can achieve much more successes.

102. By fairness we can achieve much more successes.

103. Those who act with the greatest devotion to achieve their personal goals, will achieve them much faster, more certainly and at a

much higher percentage than those who do not act with the same maximum devotion.

104. To achieve and maintain a happy marriage we need to have and use a preventive thinking.

105. To have the least possible failures in life is we need conversant as necessary to achieve personal goals, without having failures, in order to achieve them.

106. The documentation necessary to achieve the personal goals we need, we can complete from existing books or with the help of the Internet, in a very effective, cheap and operative way, etc..

107. People can become happy if they have values that help them achieve their happiness.

108. Those who will consider positive pieces of advice will have more chances to achieve more performances.

109. We can prevent more failures if we analyze our actions, their positive and negative effects, so that we and others achieve and avoid actions with negative, risky, illegal effects.

110. Most of us use our time as efficiently as we could. For this reason, through a more

efficient use of our time we can achieve much easier our personal goals.

111.   Positive thinking helps us create only positive ideas, which, in turn, help us achieve only positive deeds.

112.   Skills help us more easily achieve personal goals.

113.   As we develop more skills, the more and bigger chances we have to achieve personal goals. So, it is worth and it is necessary to develop and shape all the skills that we need in order to achieve personal goals.

114.   Selfless deeds have contributed enormously to a lot of progress and outstanding achievements in all fields of activity.

115.   By acting continuously and effectively to making a happy marriage, we shall achieve it.

116.   Applying in practice many ideas from these books, magazines, etc. you will be able to achieve much easier, much faster and even more personal goals.

117.   Those who are very receptive to all positive ideas, as opposed to those who are not, are able to achieve more successes in life.

118.   Flexibility in thinking and behavior helps us achieve much easier, much faster and a larger number of personal goals.

119.   Flexibility in thinking and behaviors is a quality necessary to achieve personal goals.

120.   Only by making a correct hierarchy, all the time, of our personal goals, according to importance and urgency, we can achieve more personal goals.

121.   The efficient organization of our personal time, continuously, day by day, helps us enormously to achieve our personal goals.

122.   Personal self-motivation, day by day, helps us achieve larger or smaller successes.

123.   The efficient organization of our personal time, day by day, helps us achieve more successes.

124.   Continuous, day by day, self-progress, helps us very much to achieve other personal goals.

125.   Spiritual self-development, continuous, day by day, helps us greatly to achieve many successes.

126.   By spiritual self-development, we can surely achieve a better life.

127. Mental self-development is necessary and required to be achieved, continuously, day by day, for as long as we live.

128. Phisical self-development and maintenance, continually, day by day, is necessary to be achieved.

129. By maintaining physical self-development, continuously, day by day, our personal goals, helps us live to achieve other personal goals.

130. Continuously, day by day, for as long as we live, it is necessary and required for us to shape and develop those personal goals that help us contribute to the development and other goals to achieve other personal goals.

131. It is necessary and required that we form and develop all the skills needed to achieve personal goals.

132. In life it is necessary to have continuously, day by day personal goals, to shape and develop, continuously, day by day, all the skills needed to achieve personal goals.

133. We can achieve skills through continuous exercises.

134. Patience very often helps us achieve greater or smaller successes.

135. In life it is necessary to enjoy every achievement, any accomplishments no matter how small if we want and act and to achieve more and greater successes.

136. Persons with many qualities are more likely to achieve more successes than those who have fewer skills.

137. Persons with many qualities have very big chances to achieve successes.

138. Each of us has many potential opportunities to assert themselves in life, it is important to discover and to achieve them.

139. He who is economical is more likely to achieve outstanding successes.

140. Those who work with dedication contribute the most to achieve the great achievements of mankind.

141. The more skilled we are in an area, the more likely we are to achieve success.

142. Optimistic people have achieved the great accomplishments of mankind.

143. If you know and apply the principles that lead us to successes we will achieve a lot and many successes.

144. Successes do not achieve themselves.

145. To have outstanding professional achievements, it is necessary to know and to apply what and how to achieve them.

146. Great realistic golas can be achieved if we apply the principles that must be applied in the actions done to achieve those objectives.

147. If we do not have goals to achieve certain successes we will not achieve them.

148. Our objectives create expectations that along with objectives and the actions we do to achieve them make us feel alive.

149. The achievement of our objective depends very much on the efficiency of our actions.

150. In the achievement of our objectives we may be helped by efficient models of actions of people who have had great successes.

151. In the achievement of our objectives we are helped very much by the art of making realistic assumptions.

152. Only if we have objectives to achieve certain successes we can actually achieve successes.

153. Our objectives in themselves only motivate us to achieve them.

154. The science of personal goals should be studied in schools and universities, etc., because it is very important for us to achieve a quality life.

155. Human resources are enormous, incalculable, a fact which can make people's lives achieve a much better quality.

156. Unfortunately, enormously many people are not concerned to find and use human knowledge that can help enormously hard to achieve a much better quality of life.

157. Our objectives gather all our energies together in order to achieve them.

158. When we have realistic goals that we believe in and act with dedication to achieve them, we are confident in our future.

159. When we have realistic goals that we believe in and act with dedication to achieve them, some of us feel happy.

160. Those who do not have realistic objectives to believe in and act with dedication to achieve them, they do not believe in the future.

161. People who live from hand to mouth do not have realistic objectives on a long term in which to believe and to whom to dedicate themselves to achieve.

162. People who live from hand to mouth do not have outstanding achievements in life.

163. Incredible facts are made mostly by people who have long-term objectives and work with dedication to achieve them.

164. Most people who perform incredible deeds had achieved that incredible objective that they believed in and to which they have dedicated themselved until they have achieved it.

165. People have already made enormously many facts that were once incredible to achieve.

166. The facts that are incredible to achieve and that have been achieved show us that many problems that many people still have at the moment can be certainly solved if they believe that they can resolve them if they act with dedication to their resolution.

167. When we achieve an objective we feel happy.

168. We can easily achieve outstanding deeds in the future if we choose, project them from now on and persevere to achieve them.

169. In most people's concerns regarding their objectives, their projects in different future aspects virtually do not exist neither in

theoretical approaches nor do they speak about plans, projects, targets achieved. This fact makes their life one lived largely at random from hand to mouth, as many are not happy in the future ahead.

170. In life it is good, it is necessary to continuously enjoy each achievement of those close to us and of any man we see. This way

171. Acting continuously and effectively to achieve positive goals we will surely achieve them.

172. It is always necessary to be effective in any situation because in this way we are able to achieve more bigger or smaller successes and a lot of enjoyment, joy, happiness.

173. Objectivity helps us become happy and achieve and maintain a happy marriage, make friends and keep them, lets us find friends and keep them, and achieve much more bigger or smaller successes.

174. Perseverance is a special quality that helps us achieve many bigger or smaller successes, face any difficulties, cavils, obstacles, achieve outstanding performances, achieve our objectives, become happy, achieve and maintain a happy marriage .

175. Knowing yourself is very necessary and very useful to us in order to achieve a happy marriage, to maintain it, to make friends and to maintain them, to use cover our qualities and flaws, etc.

176. The more we know ourselves better, the deeper, the more chances we have to obtain what we want to achieve, our objectives, to obtain successes.

177. The continuous surpassing of ourselves helps us a lot to achieve more easily our goals and it is also a guarantee of our future successes.

178. Positive thinking makes us do positive deeds, makes us be able to solve our objectives, obtain smaller or greater successes, be appreciated, respected and esteemed, achieve and maintain our happiness, a happy marriage, etc.

179. Those who have tact have more chances to achieve more joys, satisfactions and much more happiness.

180. Through marriage a woman tries to resolve her need for safety and to achieve a certain psychological comfort.

181. The need for safety and psychological comfort, a woman can only achieve through cooperation with her husband.

182.   Investment in the future needs to be made in the present to achieve our future goals.

183.   Investment in the future also means using to achieve our future objectives, financial, material, human, time resources, our own energy, other people's experience, etc..

184.   Reading and studying books is a necessity and an obligation, we need to continuously achieve our objectives.

185.   The more knowledge we have of those needed to achieve personal objectives the more likely we are to achieve our objectives.

186.   As we accumulate more positive knowledge required to achieve our objectives the more we become more able to achieve then.

187.   Those who know to use in the most efficient way 24 hours daily have the greatest chance to achieve their own happiness.

188.   Patience is a required quality both to a husband and a wife to achieve and maintain a happy and lasting marriage.

189.   Patience and the art of behaving patiently help us enormously hard to achieve personal present, future goals and ones for the future.

190. Those who have achieved many and great successes in life have a great capacity to foresee and have been forethought in many situations.

191. Our self-learning helps us incredibly much to achieve personal goals.

192. With most people who have had greater and more successes, self-learning played a decisive role. Without self-learning they would have never realized what they have achieved.

193. He who is sparing is more likely to achieve outstanding successes.

194. Kindness is a quality that helps us achieve many successes.

195. By living our lives at random we can also only achieve happiness at random.

196. Our human experience gained so far, a part of it being stored in books and on the Internet, if we study it and apply it to achieve personal objectives, we will have much greater opportunities to achieve them.

197. Our talent helps us greatly in the achievement of our personal goals.

198. The efficient management of our time helps us greatly to the achievement of our personal goals.

199. Positive thinking helps us solve positive actions. Those who do not have positive thinking have no way of achieving positive actions so they achieve negative actions.

200. Those who have creative thinking have very big chances to achieve their personal goals.

201. The more we expand the capacity of creation of creative thinking the more the number of ideas and solutions designed to achieve personal goals will increase.

202. them it is necessary then to form and develop them.

203. In order to achieve personal goals with greater opportunities it is necessary to develop the qualities needed to achieve these goals.

204. In the present, the world has sufficient resources so that more people achieve their happiness, yet people still do not use them at all or use them very little.

205. It is necessary to make people aware of all the resources and opportunities that can help them achieve their own happiness.

206. Mental self-development enormously increases our possibilities to set more and greater personal life targets and achieve them.

207. People who live in favorable circumstances also use them in life to achieve more bigger or smaller successes.

208. A personal project can bring us a lot of joy, satisfaction, fulfillment if we achieve it.

209. If we establish personal projects for whose achievement we do not have the necessary knowledge, skills, qualities and abilities, we are very likely not to achieve them.

210. Man for as long as he lives can continuously increase his capacity to create, set and achieve personal projects.

211. Continuous learning leads those who practice it to achieve many bigger or smaller successes.

212. In life we evolve very much as if we set for as long as we live a personal goal and objective to develop and move continuously, organized, planned and effective ways to achieve it.

213. In everyday life we find a lot of live models, who have as a personal goal to evolve, which have achieved many bigger or smaller

successes, joy and much happiness and satisfaction from whom we can take many effective positive behaviors to help us greatly in achieving our objective to evolve and to avoid many mistakes.

214.   All those who have achieved in life more bigger or smaller successes mostly had a constructive thinking.

215.   Those who have had a negative thinking in certain situations had many troubles, failures, conflicts in the family, some came to divorce, and they have achieved little success too.

216.   Constructive human relations, effective, harmonious ones help us greatly to achieve a beautiful life.

217.   It is necessary to promote knowledge that can make us happier, can help us to achieve much easier, faster, more efficient personal goals.

218.   The Internet can help us in the fastest way, most effectively, the more we find that existing knowledge can help us most achieve personal goals.

219.   The negative mentalities of those who have them make it very difficult to achieve efective co operations.

220. Responsibility helps us have many more opportunities to achieve personal goals.

221. The Internet helps us have many more opportunities to achieve effective co operations.

222. Altruism helps us achieve more easily more successess.

223. Using more effectively our time greatly increases our chances to achieve more and bigger successes.

224. Effective thinking helps us achieve performance.

225. Each of us must act to prevent the formation, maintenance and development of vices, since they reduce the possibilities for us to achieve our personal goals.

226. Cheerfulness helps us achieve mature love.

227. It is necessary to immediately take the necessary measures to achieve an efficient education suitable to be able to prevent crime very much by this method, which consists in carrying out an effective education appropriate to make people not want to commit crimes.

228. A woman is a fastidious being that we all want to have, whom we understand, with

whom to achieve a real mature love and a happy marriage with happy children.

229.   An active life helps us achieve easier and faster personal goals.

230.   Perseverance is a key that has helped to achieve many successes.

231.   Positive ideas help us achieve successes.

232.   The documented have much greater opportunities to achieve personal goals.

233.   We must create the conditions so that sociable people achieve their objectives as soon as their objectives have positive effects on people.

234.   The means to achieve a purpose should be legal.

235.   Positive principles help us achieve personal goals.

236.   Each spouse is required and must aim to achieve as a personal goal the harmony between him/her and the other.

237.   The exaggerated consumption of alcohol enormously harms our personal and professional achievement.

238.   The respect of the wife towards the husband is achieved through a positive behavior of

her husband towards her and the other members of his family.

239.	Personal goals, personal development helps and contributes greatly to the formation, development and achievement of other personal goals.

240.	Most of us will become happy if we set a goal to become happy and we act to achieve that goal.

241.	Our ability helps us achieve success.

242.	Sometimes patience helps us achieve success.

243.	Emotional intelligence helps us achieve greater results in work.

244.	The ability to make rapid decisions increases our chances to achieve more and greater successes.

245.	Guiding towards a goal gives us more opportunities to achieve our personal goals.

246.	The capacity of quick perception greatly increases our chances to achieve more and greater successes.

247.	Flexibility helps us a lot to us achieve a happy marriage.

248. Opening to the world greatly increases our chances to achieve personal goals.

249. New effective ways of thinking help us vey much to achieve our very special performances.

250. Optimism help us a lot to us achieve a more beautiful life.

251. Those who like very much what they do will be able to achieve efficient co-developments.

252. Positive global human solidarity helps us achieve more positive humanist actions at our local level.

253. Enthusiastic behavior greatly increases our opportunities to achieve personal goals.

254. Self-consciousness greatly increases our chances to achieve more and greater successes.

255. Sociable people are very open and have much higher chances to achieve personal goals.

256. People with an innovative spirit have much greater chances to achieve a positive future.

257. The man who is understanding has much more are much higher chances to achieve a happy marriage.

258. Energetic people have increased chances to achieve a real mature love.

259. Achieving exchanges of information helps us greatly to the achievement of a more beautiful life.

260. The trust-worthy man has much more chances to achieve a happy marriage.

261. The man willing to try new ways is much likely to achieve more personal goals.

262. People who have the capacity to argue ideas more quickly achieve true friendships.

263. The desire to succeed in life helps us a lot to achieve personal goals.

264. Those who passionately live their life have very big chances to achieve more and greater successes.

265. A quiet and reserved man has greater chances to achieve efficient co operations.

266. A man who has courage has a very big potential to self achieve in life.

267. People who are understanding achieve more social relations.

268. People who are polite achieve easier and faster social relations.

269. People who are resistant to stress have much more chances to achieve outstanding performances.

270. An emotionally stable man has much more chances to achieve outstanding performances.

271. A cooperative man in activities has a greater potential to achieve more and greater successes.

272. An understanding man has much more chances to achieve more and greater successes.

273. Continuous self perfection helps us a lot to achieve a happy marriage.

274. An intelligent man has much more possibilities to achieve efficient co operations.

275. Achieving exchanges of information helps us a lot to achieve efficient global co operations.

276. A man capable of self control in stressing situations has great chances to achieve a happy life.

277. A man who acts daily, continuously to become even more efficient has more

chances and a greater potential to achieve a happy marriage.

278. A realistic man in personal relationships has more chances and a greater potential to achieve a happy life.

279. Those who continuously expand their horizons have more and greater chances to achieve efficient co operations.

280. The richness of experience helps us a lot to achieve true friendships.

281. The ability to react with understanding helps us achieve outstanding social performances.

282. Those who are independent have achieved and achieve themselves in everyday life.

283. A more efficient management of our time helps us a lot to achieve efficient co-developments.

284. People who face contradictions have more chances to achieve more and greater successes.

285. Communicative people have more and greater chances to achieve their personal goals.

286. A disciplined man has a greater potential to achieve more and greater outstanding performances.

287. A man's need to achieve himself has continuously contributed to increasing the efficiency of human actions.

288. A full compatibility of training with the objectives helps us achieve a beautiful life.

289. Self-imposed discipline helps us a lot to achieve a true mature love.

290. Those who are preoccupied with creating an optimal cooperation in their team have great potential and great chances to achieve efficient global co operations.

291. Those who are preoccupied with creating an optimal cooperation in their team have a greater potential and a great chance to achieve personal objectives.

292. Positive personal objectives are more easily and quickly achieved by those with a greater experience.

293. Those who know how to efficiently plan their actions have greater chances to achieve personal goals.

294. True friendships help us a lot to achieve long lasting efficient co-developments.

295. The analytic spirit increases our chances and possibilities to achieve more successes.

296. An open man more easily achieves social relations.

297. The quality of sensing situations helps us a lot to achieve personal objectives.

298. Orientation towards a future world increases our ability to achieve efficient co-developments.

299. Developing the ability of listening helps us a lot to achieve our personal goals.

300. The ability to optimally adapt increases our possibilities to achieve more efficient co-developments.

Adapt

301. Education of all forms is necessary and required to adapt to the needs of people and states in the short and long term.

302. Those who adapt very easily and quickly to the requirements of the workplace have a key to obtain a job or to maintain their workplace. Try to develop your capacity and ability to adapt very quickly to the requirements of the job you want. Persevering in achieving these objectives will make you succeed. Good luck! I'm with you.

303. Adaptation is a quality and a value.

304. Adaptation helps and contributes greatly to meet more favorable opportunities.

305. It is always necessary to adapt to efficient positive changes in society.

306. Those who adapt to efficient positive changes in society will be successful.

307. Financial independence increases our ability to adapt.

308. Our ability of optimal adaptation helps us achieve more efficient co operations.

309. The ability of optimal adaptation very much increases our possibility to achieve more true friendships.

310. Efficient communication helps us adapt lives.

311. Reason helps us adapt.

312. The capacity to optimally adapt helps us have more chances to meet more favorable situations.

313. Our transformation for the better can be achieved also through the contribution of the formation, development, maintenance and usage of adapting to each situation.

314. Those who have high objectives in life mostly have the sense of adaptability.

315. Those who are remarkably gifted are adaptable.

316. People who have not succeeded in obtaining a happy marriage must develop their sense of adaptability.

317. We can prevent some failures also through the contribution of the formation, development, maintenance and usage of adaptable behaviors.

318. The force of our ideas can be enhanced also through the contribution of the formation, development, maintenance and usage of adaptable behaviors to situations that we must cope with.

319. Our transformation for the better can be achieved also through the contribution of the formation, development, maintenance and usage of adaptability to each situation.

320. In order to change our life it is necessary to form, develop, maintain and use the sense of adaptability.

321. The desire to make others happy can be accomplished through the contribution of the formation, development, maintenance and usage of the sense of adaptation.

322. The limits we have set can be overcome by the formation, development, maintenance and usage of the sense of adaptability.

323. In order to transform positive objectives into reality it is necessary to form, develop, maintain and use the sense of adaptability.

324. Loneliness can be prevented also through the contribution of the formation, development, maintenance and usage of adaptable behaviors.

325. Sometimes love makes us more adaptable.

326. Spouses must mutually adapt to one another.

327. Wise spouses adapt to one another.

328. Spouses that adapt to one another will have a long lasting marriage.

329. Our chances of becoming happy increase if we are adaptable.

330. In order to follow and transform our personal goals into reality, it is necessary to also form, develop, maintain and use our adaptable behavior.

331. Adaptation helps us become loving.

332. Continuous self perfection helps us become adaptable.

333. In order to prevent failures it is necessary to also form, develop, maintain and use adaptable behavior.

334. Adaptation helps us become wise.

335. We can contribute to the achievement of our greatest accomplishments also through the contribution of the formation, development, maintenance and usage of adaptable behavior.

336. Adaptation must be encouraged.

337. Confidence in ourselves helps us become adaptable.

338. Continuous self-control helps us become adaptable.

339. Acting efficiently helps us become adaptable.

340. In order to rise up once again for the first time for the who knows what time it is necessary to also form, develop, maintain and use adaptable behavior.

341. Adaptation helps us achieve more efficient co operations.

342. Our future can be projected and achieved also through the contribution of the formation, development, maintenance and usage of adaptable behavior.

48

343. Adaptation helps us become happier.

344. Self-imposed discipline helps us become adaptable.

345. The necessary qualities in achieving personal goals can be formed, developed, maintained and used also through the contribution of the formation, development, maintenance and usage of adaptable behavior.

346. Adaptation helps us achieve more records.

347. Responsibility helps us become adaptable.

348. The force of our ideas can be augmented also through the contribution of the formation, development, maintenance and usage of adaptable behavior.

349. Adaptation helps us achieve personal goals.

350. The radical transformation for the better of our life can be achieved also through the formation, development, maintenance and usage of adaptable behavior.

351. Adaptation helps us maintain happiness.

352. Aspiring towards a more meaningful life can also be achieved through the formation, development, maintenance and usage of adaptable behavior.

353.   Will helps us become adaptable.

354.   Adaptation helps us become happy.

355.   Adaptation must be a model.

356.   We can prevent the falling apart of a happy marriage also through the contribution of the formation, development, maintenance and usage of adaptable behavior.

357.   Communication helps us become adaptable.

358.   Creativity helps us become adaptable.

359.   Adaptation helps us maintain optimism.

360.   Obtaining more and greater successes can be achieved also through the contribution of the formation, development, maintenance, usage of an adaptable behavior.

361.   Adaptation helps us maintain productivity.

362.   Adaptation helps us become loved.

363.   Adaptation helps us become more loving.

364.   The limits of achievement imposed by ourselves in our mind at a given moment can be overcome or eliminated also through the contribution of the formation, development, maintenance and usage of adaptable behavior.

365. The solutions to the problems we have or that we want to solve can be found also through the contribution of the formation, development, maintenance and usage of adaptable behavior.

366. We can prevent some failures also through the contribution of the formation, development, maintenance and usage of adaptable behavior.

367. Problems cannot be solved by the ideas that created them but also through the contribution of the formation, development, maintenance and usage of adaptable behavior.

368. Adaptation helps us become more cautious.

369. Stress can be prevented also through the formation, development, maintenance and usage of adaptable behavior.

370. Adaptation helps us achieve more favorable chances.

371. In order to escape poverty it is necessary to also form, develop, maintain and use adaptable behavior.

372. Continuous self-motivation helps us become adaptable.

373. Adaptation helps us become enthusiastic.

374. In achieving our successes a contribution is also brought by the formation, development, maintenance and usage of adaptable behavior.

375. Adaptation helps us maintain tolerance.

376. Hope helps us become adaptable.

377. Adaptation helps us become more practical.

378. Rather than lamenting that we do not have successes it is more useful to also form, develop, maintain and use adaptable behavior.

379. Adaptation helps us maintain enthusiasm.

380. Cherishing oneself helps us become adaptable.

381. Adaptation must be used.

382. Adaptation helps us become productive.

383. Optimism helps us become adaptable.

384. Adaptation helps us maintain wisdom.

385. We can overcome the difficulties that we must overcome also through the help of the formation, development, maintenance and usage of adaptable behavior.

386. Adaptation helps us become humane.

387. Hopes can be created also through the contribution of the formation, development, maintenance and usage of adaptable behavior.

388. Adaptation helps us become more optimistic.

389. We can form, develop and maintain the state of being ourselves also through the contribution of the formation, development, maintenance and usage of an adaptable behavior.

390. Adaptation helps us become more pleasant.

391. In order to prevent not achieving our personal goals, it is necessary to also form, develop, maintain and use our adaptable behavior.

392. The obstacles that prevent us from achieving our personal goals can be surpassed also through the contribution of the formation, development, maintenance and usage of adaptable behavior.

393. Adaptation helps us become efficient.

394. Adaptation must be imitated.

395. Positive experience can be achieved also through the contribution of the formation,

development, maintenance and usage of adaptable behavior.

396. Adaptation must be developed.

397. Some mistakes can be prevented also through the contribution of the formation, development, maintenance and usage of adaptable behavior.

398. Our happiness depends a lot also on the formation, development, maintenance and usage of adaptable behavior.

Affection

399. Each of us needs to receive affection.

400. Both spouses who have children need and must provide the warmth and affection required by children up to 18 years and older to ensure the safety of the family.

401. There are people who become ill in order to receive affection.

402. Affectionate women more easily achieve happy marriages.

Agreeable

403. People who are continuously well intentioned are agreeable.

404. We can form, develop and maintain the state of being ourselves also through the contribution of the formation, development, maintenance and usage of an agreeable behavior.

405. Some mistakes can be prevented also through the contribution of the formation, development, maintenance and usage of agreeable behavior.

406. Self-imposed discipline helps us become agreeable.

407. We can become stronger and we can not allow ourselves to be influenced by the world also through the contribution of the formation, development, maintenance and usage of agreeable behavior.

408. The self efficient use of our time helps us become agreeable.

409. Acting efficiently helps us become agreeable.

410. Communication helps us become agreeable.

411. Confidence in ourselves helps us become agreeable.

412. Stress can be prevented also through the formation, development, maintenance and usage of agreeable behavior.

413.   We can contribute to the achievement of our greatest accomplishments also through the contribution of the formation, development, maintenance and usage of agreeable behavior.

414.   Problems cannot be solved by the ideas that created them but also through the contribution of the formation, development, maintenance and usage of agreeable behavior.

415.   Our resistance to changing for the better can be overcome also through the contribution of the formation, development, maintenance and usage of agreeable behavior.

416.   Optimism helps us become agreeable.

417.   In order to rise up once again for the first time for the who knows what time it is necessary to also form, develop, maintain and use agreeable behavior.

418.   Continuous self-motivation helps us become agreeable.

419.   Aspiring towards a more meaningful life can also be achieved through the formation, development, maintenance and usage of agreeable behavior.

420.   Our future can be projected and achieved also through the contribution of the

formation, development, maintenance and usage of agreeable behavior.

421.   Will helps us become agreeable.

422.   Hopes can be created also through the contribution of the formation, development, maintenance and usage of agreeable behavior.

423.   Continuously making ourselves efficient helps us become agreeable.

424.   The necessary qualities in achieving personal goals can be formed, developed, maintained and used also through the contribution of the formation, development, maintenance and usage of agreeable behavior.

425.   We can prevent some failures also through the contribution of the formation, development, maintenance and usage of agreeable behavior.

426.   Responsibility helps us become agreeable.

427.   Continuous self perfection helps us become agreeable.

428.   The obstacles that prevent us from achieving our personal goals can be surpassed also through the contribution of

the formation, development, maintenance and usage of agreeable behavior.

429.   Cherishing oneself helps us become agreeable.

430.   In achieving our successes a contribution is also brought by the formation, development, maintenance and usage of agreeable behavior.

431.   The limits of achievement imposed by ourselves in our mind at a given moment can be overcome or eliminated also through the contribution of the formation, development, maintenance and usage of agreeable behavior.

432.   Our own happiness can be achieved and maintained also through the contribution of the formation, development, maintenance and usage of agreeable behavior.

433.   Wisdom helps us become agreeable.

434.   We can overcome the difficulties that we must overcome also through the help of the formation, development, maintenance and usage of agreeable behavior.

435.   In order to escape poverty it is necessary to also form, develop, maintain and use agreeable behavior.

436. We can prevent the falling apart of a happy marriage also through the contribution of the formation, development, maintenance and usage of agreeable behavior.

437. Our happiness depends a lot also on the formation, development, maintenance and usage of agreeable behavior.

438. Creativity helps us become agreeable.

439. Positive experience can be achieved also through the contribution of the formation, development, maintenance and usage of agreeable behavior.

440. In order to prevent failures it is necessary to also form, develop, maintain and use agreeable behavior.

441. Rather than lamenting that we do not have successes it is more useful to also form, develop, maintain and use agreeable behavior.

442. Hope helps us become agreeable.

Alone

443. When you are discriminated take all necessary measures to end discrimination and avoid the possiblity to get in a position to be discriminated against. You are not

alone. Call institutions that are empowered. Good luck.

444. Those who are alone can get rid of loneliness by applying the principle of cooperation.

445. Young people feel better in a community, a group than alone.

446. Regardless of how we live, it is not worth it to be alone which makes our life less beautiful.

Ambition

447. The people's ambition to act efficiently has contributed a lot to achieving the general good.

448. The ambitions man has a great potential to achieve efficient co operations.

449. Ambitions can be formed and developed.

450. People's ambition to act efficiently will lead to the achievement of many social relations.

451. The ambition to act efficiently of people helps them and contributes to achieving efficient co-developments.

452. Negative ambitions are very harmful sometimes.

453. Positive ambition must always be encouraged.

454. Maintaining positive ambition must be a personal objective of ours for as long as we live.

455. Positive ambition has achieved many performances.

456. Positive ambition prevents many negative facts.

Appreciate

457. Luxury must not be appreciated.

458. Selflessness is a model of positive behavior that is necessary to appreciate.

459. Positive actions should be appreciated.

460. We must reward and appreciate selfless deeds, at their just value.

461. We need to appreciate and support selfless ideas, to promote, to make them become facts.

462. Positive facts need to be appreciated.

463. For the sake of ourselves and of others, of human society, it is necessary and

mandatory to appreciate and respect positive thinking.

464.   For our sake and that of others, of human society, it is necessary and required to appreciate, promote and apply positive ideas.

465.   A skillful man is appreciated.

466.   A man with qualities is appreciated.

467.   Many of us do not appreciate health at its just value.

468.   Politeness makes us more appreciated.

469.   He who is quiet is appreciated by most people.

470.   I esteem women very much, appreciate and respect them very much for what they are, for the special qualities that they have.

471.   Often, many men do not respect, do not appreciate, do not help women enough as they have to.

472.   Inner spiritual beauty makes a woman special, permanently young and a magnet for many men, this makes her much more appreciated, respected and esteemed.

473.   Perseverance gives us power, strenghtens us, makes us honorable, respected and appreciated.

474.   Men need to appreciate, respect all the qualities of women no matter what the situation is, even in this situation when these have more qualities than them.

475.   The husband who has a wife with more qualities than he does needs to be proud of her, to respect her, appreciate and support her, help her use her qualities for her sake, their children's sake and her husband's sake.

476.   Positive thinking makes us do positive deeds, makes us be able to solve our objectives, obtain smaller or greater successes, be appreciated, respected and esteemed, achieve and maintain our happiness, a happy marriage, etc.

477.   There are certain situations in marriage when women have more and more qualities and greater achievements than men. In these circumstances the man should not feel inferior, complexed, frustated, moody, disturbed by the situation, etc.. but instead he should see the good side of the situation, to enjoy a lot of the qualities and achievements of his wife, to be proud of her, to stimulate, appreciate and respect her more and assist her in achieving her

objectives, to help her when she need his help and he can give it to her.

478.   Reliability makes us be more appreciated.

479.   Some employees unproperly appreciated will quit that job.

480.   Those who have performances are very appreciated. Persevere and you can have performance and be very appreciated. Good luck.

481.   The person who has an active life is appreciated and known.

482.   Perseverent people are appreciated.

483.   The man who has legal principles must be appreciated.

484.   Positive principles help us be more appreciated.

485.   The man who has a wife with several qualities should appreciate her more.

486.   A man must always appreciate the qualities of women.

487.   As we do more good with more opportunities we have to be appreciated.

488. People with skills do not envy the achievements of others but appreciate them to just their value.

489. Intelligence must always be supported, promoted, appreciated, respected and rewarded.

490. Cheerfulness must always be supported, promoted, appreciated, respected and rewarded.

491. The sense of objectivity must be appreciated.

492. A happy marriage is something invaluable, unable to transliterate, which many of us know and we do not want to appreciate its just value, thus making a huge mistake and a very bad one.

493. Co-development makes us become more appreciated.

494. He who is disciplined is appreciated, respected and rewarded.

495. Bad faith is not appreciated by anyone.

496. Senselessness is a much unappreciated behavior.

497. The optimistic ones are appreciated.

498. Conceit is never fully appreciated.

499.   Self- control is a quality very necessary and very appreciated for shared living.

500.   Those who are not dedicated are not appreciated.

501.   Sincerity is a highly appreciated quality.

502.   Those who do not properly appreciate honesty are not humane.

503.   Promptness is appreciated by all of us.

504.   There are men who appreciate more the moral beauty than the physical beauty of a woman.

505.   The work of correct journalists must be supported by all of us, appreciated and rewarded at its just value, according to the case.

506.   Some journalists risk their work, freedom, health, life for us to offer society and people as much as they can but we do not unfortunately know and do not appreciate them, reward them enough for what they do for us.

507.   They deserve to be appreciated, honored, respected and rewarded, all those journalists who do not act by order to unjustly hit some people, or groups of people.

508.   Co- development makes us become more appreciated.

509.   The activity of voluntarism must be encouraged and appreciated at its just value.

510.   Kindness makes us appreciated.

511.   Those who recognize other people's actions are people who are appreciated by their collaborators

512.   Reliability makes us be much more appreciated.

513.   Self control must always be promoted, sustained, appreciated, respected and rewarded.

514.   Work must always be promoted, sustained, appreciated, respected and rewarded.

515.   Those with the sense of responsibility must be appreciated, promoted, supported and rewarded.

516.   A very sociable man is much appreciated.

517.   Those willing to try new ways must be appreciated.

518.   A man who is full of energy and active must be appreciated.

519.   Careful people must be appreciated.

520.   Prejudices must not be appreciated.

521.   Independence must always be promoted, appreciated, respected and rewarded.

522.   The sense of responsibility needs to be appreciated, promoted, supported and respected.

523.   He who is very conscious is much appreciated.

524.   Those who are capable of self control in stressing situations must be appreciated, promoted, sustained and rewarded.

525.   Those with a greater resistance to stress must be appreciated.

526.   Men who have wives who earn more than they do need to appreciate them very much.

527.   Honor must be promoted, supported, appreciated, respected and rewarded.

528.   Courage must always be promoted, supported, appreciated, respected and rewarded.

529.   Polite people are respected, appreciated and esteemed.

530. Communicative people are appreciated, respected, esteemed and rewarded.

531. Magnanimity must be respected, appreciated, esteemed and rewarded.

532. Efficient human communication must be appreciated, promoted, sustained and rewarded.

533. Those who are enthusiastic must be appreciated, promoted, supported and rewarded.

534. Those who are very conscious need to be promoted, appreciated, supported and rewarded.

535. People who inspire trust must be appreciated.

536. People with the sense of discipline must be appreciated.

537. Those with the sense of objectivity must be appreciated.

538. The state of certainty must be appreciated.

539. Magnanimity is a quality that makes us very appreciated by people.

540. Constructive thinking must be appreciated.

541. The majority of those with the ability to react with understanding are appreciated.

542. People who are not careful with others must not be appreciated.

543. Those who only solve problems through constructive methods must be appreciated.

544. Solving problems through positive methods must be appreciated.

545. People who have success appreciate their success.

546. The need to succeed must be appreciated.

547. The majority of those who have the ability to react with understanding must be appreciated.

548. People who know how to motivate must be appreciated.

549. Those who live their life passionately and not at random must be appreciated.

550. The majority of those involved in many new projects must be appreciated.

551. The inner beauty of a woman is more and more appreciated by man.

552. Man needs to appreciate inner beauty in women as a priority.

553. Sometimes we sacrifice ourselves for many people but few of them appreciate the gesture.

554. A man with many qualities is highly appreciated.

555. Kindness makes us be appreciated.

556. The inner beauty of a woman is more and more appreciated by more men.

557. The more a man has more qualities the more appreciated he will be.

558. A man who is willing at any time to help someone is highly appreciated and loved by people.

559. Responsibility must always be promoted, supported, appreciated, respected and rewarded.

560. Tact must always be promoted, supported, appreciated, respected and rewarded.

561. A giving man is loved and appreciated by people.

562. The preference for uncontrolled positive activism must be appreciated, promoted, supported and rewarded.

563. The sense of responsibility must be appreciated, promoted, supported and rewarded.

564. The ability to dissociate emotions from responsibilities must be appreciated, promoted, supported and rewarded.

565. Those who cherish their collaborators must be appreciated, promoted and supported.

566. A low tolerance for personal imperfections must be appreciated, promoted, supported and rewarded.

567. Not assuring personal freedom must not be appreciated.

568. Those who willingly expand their positive experience must be appreciated.

569. A neat aspect must always be promoted, supported, appreciated, respected and rewarded.

570. A broad horizon must always be promoted, supported, appreciated, respected and rewarded.

571. An honest man is appreciated, respected and esteemed by other people.

572. The need to succeed must be appreciated.

573. The majority of those who have the ability to react with understanding must be appreciated.

574. People who know how to motivate must be appreciated.

575. Those who live their life passionately and not at random must be appreciated.

576. The majority of those involved in many new projects must be appreciated.

577. The inner beauty of a woman is more and more appreciated by man.

578. Man needs to appreciate inner beauty in women as a priority.

579. Sometimes we sacrifice ourselves for many people but few of them appreciate the gesture.

580. A man with many qualities is highly appreciated.

581. Kindness makes us be appreciated.

582. The inner beauty of a woman is more and more appreciated by more men.

583. The more a man has more qualities the more appreciated he will be.

584.   A man who is willing at any time to help someone is highly appreciated and loved by people.

585.   Responsibility must always be promoted, supported, appreciated, respected and rewarded.

586.   Tact must always be promoted, supported, appreciated, respected and rewarded.

587.   A giving man is loved and appreciated by people.

588.   The preference for uncontrolled positive activism must be appreciated, promoted, supported and rewarded.

589.   The sense of responsibility must be appreciated, promoted, supported and rewarded.

590.   The ability to dissociate emotions from responsibilities must be appreciated, promoted, supported and rewarded.

591.   Those who cherish their collaborators must be appreciated, promoted and supported.

592.   A low tolerance for personal imperfections must be appreciated, promoted, supported and rewarded.

593.   Not assuring personal freedom must not be appreciated.

594. Those who willingly expand their positive experience must be appreciated.

595. A neat aspect must always be promoted, supported, appreciated, respected and rewarded.

596. A broad horizon must always be promoted, supported, appreciated, respected and rewarded.

597. An honest man is appreciated, respected and esteemed by other people.

598. People who are used to carry out the activities they have started must be appreciated, promoted, supported and rewarded.

599. A quiet man is very appreciated, esteemed and respected.

600. The state of nervosity must not be appreciated.

601. Assuring personal freedom must be appreciated.

602. Those who discover unique ways to work efficiently for a better life must be appreciated.

603. People who do not have hopes in order to create hopes need to connect with people who appreciate their collaborators.

604. Most of those who know how to prevent possible mistakes must be appreciated.

605. A positive conception of life must be appreciated.

606. Those who know that discipline is one of the key of dreams must be appreciated.

607. People who have the ability to take rapid quality decisions must be appreciated.

608. Those who control circumstances must be appreciated.

609. An enterprising spirit must be appreciated.

610. People who control their emotions must be appreciated.

611. Those who have the ability to consciously choose must be appreciated.

612. Those who have had better economical and social conditions during their evolution must be appreciated.

613. Spouses who appreciate each other have greater chances to achieve a happy family.

614. Those who do well for others must be appreciated.

615. Positive ideas must always be appreciated.

616. Responsibility makes us be more appreciated.

617. The desire to succeed in life must be appreciated.

618. All positive deeds must be appreciated.

619. Positive actions must be appreciated.

620. Consciousness makes us more appreciated at work.

621. The efficient management of our personal time must be appreciated.

622. Polite people must be appreciated.

623. Responsibility always needs to be appreciated.

624. The polite man must be appreciated.

625. The efficient human communication must be appreciated.

626. Those who control surroundings must be appreciated.

627. We must permanently appreciate in others what is good for them.

628. Positive ambition must always be appreciated.

629. Optimistic attitude must be appreciated.

630. The ability to change our less efficient ideas with others that are more efficient must be appreciated.

631. Efficient inter human relations must be appreciated.

632. We must always appreciate our friends' positive deeds.

633. Hopes must be appreciated.

634. The hopes of others must be appreciated.

635. Imagination must be appreciated.

636. Communication between friends must be appreciated.

637. We must appreciate those who have achievements.

638. We must appreciate all of those who have positive actions.

639. Life is a lot more pleasant when your positive actions are appreciated.

640. True friends appreciate each other.

641. True friendships must be appreciated.

642. Creativity must be appreciated.

643. Creative qualities must be appreciated.

644. Ingenuity must be appreciated.

645. Affectionate manifestations must be appreciated by spouses.

646. Lovers must appreciate each other when they talk about their own emotions.

647. Spouses must appreciate each other when they talk about their own emotions.

648. Love gestures must be appreciated by spouses.

649. Spouses must appreciate one another's love gestures.

Argue

650. People who have the capacity to argue ideas more quickly achieve true friendships.

651. Those who have argued that their illegalities can not be discovered are terribly wrong.

652. Arguments undermine the very tranquility of the one who argues.

653. Life is a lot more beautiful when we do not argue.

654. We must never argue.

Arrogance

655. Arrogance is a brake, is an obstacle to achieving many friendships.

656. Those who have high objectives in life mostly have the spirit of arrogance.

657. Arrogance between spouses is unacceptable.

Assume

658. Those who voluntarily assume some risks only when they have an increased chance to reach their objectives have a higher potential and more chances to achieve more and greater successes.

659. People who have success voluntarily assume only when they have spontaneous successes the achievement of the goal.

660. Those who voluntarily assume certain risks when they have the increased chance of obtaining their objective are engines of progress in all areas of activity.

661. Those who voluntarily assume certain risks only when they have the increased chance of reaching their objective become more effective.

662.   Those who voluntarily assume certain risks only when they have an increased chance of reaching their objective must and are worth being appreciated, promoted, supported and rewarded.

663.   In order to prevent failures it is necessary to form, develop, maintain and use the ability to assume risks.

664.   A radical transformation for the better of our life can be achieved also through the contribution of the formation, development, maintenance and usage of the ability to assume risks.

665.   In order to prevent failures it is necessary to form, develop, maintain and use the ability to assume the risks.

666.   True friendships assume fairness between friends.

Attention

667.   The attention given to justice by the society is enormously small as compared to the importance of justice to the society and people.

668.   If we have children, in order to prevent divorce and its negative effects, it is necessary for scientists to pay more

attention to studying family relationships and family.

669. The lack of attention can create major damage very often.

670. Accidents sometimes are caused by abstraction. So, pay attention to actions.

671. A charming man attracts the attention of many women.

672. A charming woman draws the attention of many men.

673. Inattention can often have very big negative effects.

674. To achieve quality actions to become happy and maintain our happiness, it is necessary that every time we act to focus totally on that action, to be careful in everything we do. Any little distraction can have grater or smaller negative effects on our happiness. Because of this, our happiness totally depends on our overall happiness and on the quality of actions which we achieve, on the concentration and attention with which we perform them.

675. Lack of attention can create very large damages very often concomitant stop or delay the final achievement of personal goals.

676.   Most women and men want a happy
        marriage, but unfortunately they do too little,
        they give too little time, too little attention to
        achieve and to maintain it. If, instead, they
        do all that is necessary to achieve and
        maintain a happy marriage, they will surely
        make it. We wish you success confident that
        you will be able to build and maintain a
        happy marriage. Good luck again.

677.   Most of us do too little to maintain our
        health. This is a very big mistake which
        costs us many lives, reducing years of life,
        one or more diseases with more suffering,
        sometimes a happy marriage, good
        relationships with children, etc.. Attention to
        your health. Take sufficient care of your
        health. Good luck.

678.   Sometimes inattention can lead directly to
        the grave. Warning.

679.   The objective of personal planning for our
        actions continuously, day by day, for as long
        as we live, contributes greatly to achieving
        our other goals. It deserves to get our
        attention because of its importance. Good
        luck.

680.   The personal goal of effectively organizing
        our actions continuously, day by day, for as
        long as we live, contributes greatly to
        achieving other of our personal objectives. It

deserves to receive the necessary attention, because of its importance. Good luck.

681.	Increasing the ability to focus our attention helps contribute to the increasing of our efficiency in what we do.

682.	Each of us needs to pay attention to the development required for a creative thinking.

683.	Each parent is required to give the time and attention necessary to the education, guidance, consultation and raising of children.

684.	Increasing the ability to focus attention helps us and contributes to achieving independence.

685.	Each of us needs to pay the attention and time needed to develop preventive thinking.

686.	There are still too many parents who do not give the attention and time needed to educate and raise their children.

687.	Illegal actions can never be perfectly covered so as not to be discovered. So attention, you would better not do it.

688.	Think of yourselves when you do something legal or illegal even if the guilty one can go to prison. You had better pay extra attention;

it does not require great efforts and is not worth doing many years in prisons.

689.   Discovered illegal actions create very large damages often to those who have done them. So, pay much attention, better think it over a hundred times than face the negative effects of an illegal action that you rushed to make. What do you think?

690.   Life is too beautiful for a part of it to be spent in prison for negligence or lack of attention.

691.   If we are distracted in what we do at any time one or more unpleasant surprises may occur. So pay much attention.

692.   The increased ability to focus our attention helps us contribute greatly to achieving more fulfillments.

693.   Each of us needs to pay attention to the development thinking in the long term.

694.   Illegal actions can destroy happy marriages. So pay much attention.

695.   People who are not paying attention when they are driving vehicles can go at any time to prison, because at any time they can make a stupid accident.

696.   Increasing the ability to focus our attention helps us maintain a happy marriage.

697. Each of us needs to pay attention when necessary and appropriate to the development of human thought.

698. States do not give the necessary attention to create work places because they lack the will needed.

699. States give very small attention to the training and development of positive thinking.

700. Often, unfortunately, we make many inefficient operations that make us sick because of an idea or more belonging to us. So pay attention to the ideas you have.

701. Before you put your ideas into practice, review them with the highest professionalism and attention to discover if they are wrong or not. Good luck.

702. The increased capacity of concentration of our attention helps us and contributes to increasing our efficiency in what we do.

703. Each of us is necessary to pay the attention necessary to developing our creative thinking.

704. Each parent is required to give the time and attention necessary for the education, guidance, consultation of raising children.

705.   Each of us must give the attention and time needed to form and develop continuously our creative thinking.

706.   Meditations make us give more attention and time in all that concerns us.

707.   Employees who go to work drunk are first on the lists of redundancy. Attention amateurs.

708.   Negative feelings damage us and others. Attention not to make them, maintain and develop them.

709.   Unfortunately, the majority of men give too little attention and too little time to achieving a happy marriage.

710.   It is certain that if people give the attention and time needed to achieve a happy marriage they will succeed in achieving more happy marriages.

711.   It is certain that our life can be much more beautiful if we give the necessary attention and time to achieving and maintaining a beautiful life.

712.   Humanist scientific knowledge, human living experience, stored in books, on the Internet, in the media, human qualities allow the achievement of an incredibly high number of happy marriages, but, unfortunately, many people do not give the time and the attention

necessary to achieving and maintaining a happy marriage.

713. How can you achieve and maintain a happy marriage if you know do not advocate it the time and the attention needed?

714. It is certain that if spouses would give the attention and time needed to maintain a happy marriage they would succeed and there would be less unhappy marriages and divorces.

715. Human attention is what increases our contact.

716. Gaining the attention of the other is sometimes a big achievement.

717. Gaining the attention of buyers is an objective that is hard to reach but not impossible.

718. Unfortunately, parents never give the necessary attention and time to their children.

719. Each parent needs and must give the necessary attention and time to his children.

720. Unfortunately enormously many people do not to give the importance, the attention or the time needed for a true marriage.

721. Small attentions contribute to maintaining true friendships.

722. The self-control of our behaviors helps us a lot to prevent lack of attention.

723. A great capacity of drawing attention helps us become understanding.

Attitude

724. Young people from all of the world's states should not be negligent, careless, passive, inactive, non-participative in taking decisions that concern them, their present and future, but to take part in decision-making in local councils, central parliaments, governments and other state and non-state institutions, and use all their capacities, abilities, skills, attitudes, knowledge, energy, commitment and desire to assert and achieve great deeds, to create a more humane, more righteous, more happy, with less trouble world.

725. Where necessary, it is good to change attitudes and behavior because only so we can achieve happiness.

726. It is always needed to develop capacities, skills, qualities and attitudes, but we need the development of our personality, it is necessary to have this as a personal objective.

727. The creative attitudes that we do not have we must form to help us become more creative.

728. People who have a positive attitude are preferred by employers. A positive attitude is a quality and a key to obtaining the work we desire and to keep us as an employee. If you do not have a positive attitude, it is no problem, you can learn if you want, it can be learned easily. Good luck! I'm with you.

729. The orientation towards everything new is a creative attitude that helps us a lot to achieve personal goals.

730. If a person does not have creative attitude, a shift towards everything new, he can shape and develop it.

731. Confidence in our own forces is a creative attitude that helps us and contributes greatly to achieve our personal goals.

732. A person who has no creative attitude, confidence in his own forces, he can auto-shape it, develop and maintain it for life.

733. The diversity of interests is a creative attitude that helps us a lot to achieve personal goals.

734. A person who has no creative attitude, diversity of interests can auto-shape,

develop and maintain it for as long as he lives.

735.   Our orientation towards a very distant future is a creative attitude that helps us a lot to achieve our personal goals.

736.   The ability to use the completion of ideas is a creative attitude that helps us a lot to achieve our personal goals.

737.   A person who does not have the attitude of complete creative ideas in the state that it can be useful, can also auto shape it, develop and maintain it for as long as he lives. Good luck.

738.   The diversity of our interests is a creative attitude that helps us a lot to be more creative.

739.   The diversity of our interests is a creative attitude that helps us a lot more to resolve problems more quickly.

740.   A person who has no creative attitude oriented towards the future can auto-shape, develop and maintain it for as long as he lives. Good luck.

741.   The creative attitude oriented towards the future helps us very much to resolve more problems more quickly.

742. The ability to mobilize is a creative attitude that helps us become more creative.

743. We can create a beautiful life for ourselves if we have creative attitudes.

744. We should always prevent suicidal behavior, attitudes, ideas and thoughts.

745. The state is required to set up specialized services for the prevention and elimination of suicidal behaviors, attitudes, ideas and thoughts in order to reduce to a maximum the possibility of suicides.

746. We can make our life more beautiful and if we have creative attitudes.

747. We always need to prevent suicidal behavior, attitudes, ideas and suicidal thoughts.

748. It is needed to establish specialized services for the prevention and elimination of suicidal behaviors, attitudes, ideas and thoughts to reduce to a maximum possible suicides.

749. Creative attitudes, qualities and capacities must be rewarded.

750. By developing new abilities, new attitudes and new qualities we will increase our chances very much to achieve personal goals.

751. Each of us can be free in thought only due to preconceptions, superstitions and the absence of the necessary knowledge and of creative attitudes.

752. Creative attitudes contribute a lot in spiritual self development.

753. A great capacity of using attitudes helps us become loving.

754. Our positive attitude towards life helps us achieve more successes.

Attraction

755. The hugging of lovers increases their mutual sexual attraction.

756. The caresses of lovers increase their mutual sexual attraction.

757. The comforting of lovers increases their mutual sexual attraction.

758. The kissing of lovers increases their mutual sexual attraction.

759. The tenderness of lovers increases their sexual attraction.

760. Caresses between lovers also create physical attraction.

Bad

761. If we have problems it is not necessary to be in a bad mood. Problems are problems, and we deal with them in the most serious way, even if we are in a good mood.

762. Frequent sorrows are bad for our health.

763. He who is accused in bad faith, illegally, has long suffered unjustly.

764. By allowing what is bad can sometimes cause us much harm.

765. True friends are those who wish you well, cooperate with you when you need to, who are there by your side in every good and bad situation. They are those people who do not leave in exceptional circumstances, the most difficult ones of your life.

766. Unfortunately, incredibly many people do nothing or almost nothing to achieve their own happiness. However they do something bad, they lament the fact that they are not happy, they do not have luck, they are absurdly jealous of those who are happy forgetting that they are the only ones guilty for not being happy (in most cases) because firstly they do nothing to be happy.

767. When we think constructively not destructively, we think this helps us prevent

many mistakes, failures, accidents, divorces, misfortunes, conflicts, which are bad, harmful to us or others.

768. A happy marriage is something invaluable, unable to transliterate, which many of us know and we do not want to appreciate its just value, thus making a huge mistake and a very bad one.

769. When the husband behaves badly with his wife and hates her, he alienates her from him.

770. Bad faith breaks many true friendships.

771. Irritations happen whether we are bad or good, but they do not solve any problem, but instead some can greatly complicate and even create other problems.

772. Insulting harms the one who does so sometimes very badly.

773. When a husband treats his wife badly he pushes her away very much.

774. Even if we reach the situation of despair we can very easily get rid of it most of the times because life was given to us to live it with the goods and bads, for we have the qualities necessary but we have to use them effectively.

775.   The state of anger is bad for our health.

776.   A lie, defined truth through definite court decision, cannot become the truth, because the definite court decision is a false and a felony resulted from many felonies committed by the judge who, in bad faith, has illegally turned a lie into the truth through an illegal and false definite court order.

777.   Bad luck is made by each of us.

778.   Continuous arguments are bad for our health.

779.   Repeated argumentative talks can be bad for our health.

780.   Argumentative talks are very bad for marriages.

781.   Argumentative talks are very bad for love.

782.   Argumentative talks are very bad for a friendship.

783.   It is normal that spouses are sometimes in a bad mood.

784.   Being morose is bad for the marriage.

785.   The annoyances of spouses in a marriage are bad for the marriage.

786. There are situations in which we can be happy but not feel happy because we think, in a bad way, that we are not happy.

787. Each woman has the need to be understood why she is in a bad mood.

788. Prevention against bad people helps us achieve more pleasant surprises.

789. Prevention against bad people helps us achieve much good luck.

Bastard

790. He who is a bastard chases people away from him.

791. He who is a bastard harms himself with his blackness.

792. In addition to being a bastard a bastard man hasn't at least any common sense many times.

793. Bastards are always trying to take advantage of those who are powerless.

794. Thanklessness makes those who are bastards be rejected by the others.

795. Those who take advantage of those who are powerless are bastards.

Beautiful

796.   Most of us do not have as a permanent
         objective the achievement of a good life and
         we are not even seriously concerned to
         reach it. So how can we have a beautiful
         life?

797.   Life can be more beautiful if we set as a
         priority the objective of achieving a good life
         and if we continuously work to achieve this
         objective.

798.   Life for many of us can be more beautiful if
         we are concerned with making it more
         beautiful.

799.   To make others happy though your own
         happiness is the most beautiful occupation
         in the world.

800.   Life is very beautiful and pleasant to us if we
         make it nice and pleasant.

801.   Women very often make a men's life more
         beautiful, with many joys and many
         satisfactions. Unfortunately some men do
         not know how to assess the fair value of
         these particular facts of many women.

802.   Our life becomes much more beautiful, more
         full of joy, happiness and satisfaction as we
         have more real friends and as we know

better how to cooperate with them to achieve, when necessary, our goals.

803. Life is more beautiful when we have real friends.

804. Life to very many people could become more beautiful if they would set a personal goal to achieve a more beautiful life, and if they would continuously act for as long as they live to achieve this objective.

805. In life it is necessary to achieve as many true friends as possible because they make our life more beautiful.

806. Those who have as a personal objective the harmonious development of their character will succeed in life and achieve a more beautiful life than those who do not have among their personal goals the harmonious development of their personality.

807. Constructive human relations, effective, harmonious ones help us greatly to achieve a beautiful life.

808. We can make our life a lot more beautiful as we have an education most appropriate for us to achieve it.

809. Psychological balance helps achieve a more beautiful life.

810. Life will be much more beautiful if we know how to achieve a happy marriage.

811. We can create a more beautiful life if we have more experience.

812. True friendship makes life more beautiful for those two friends or for that group of friends.

813. Optimism help us a lot to us achieve a more beautiful life.

814. Achieving exchanges of information helps us greatly to the achievement of a more beautiful life.

815. The man oriented towards a very remote future has more and much greater chances to achieve a beautiful life for himself.

816. A man with self control knows how to realize a more beautiful life.

817. Very giving people ready to interrupt their own road to help others have greater chances to achieve a more beautiful life.

818. Those with the sense of responsibility manage to achieve a more beautiful life.

819. The majority of people with the sense of responsibility manage to achieve a beautiful life.

820. Those who are enthusiastic have a greater ability to achieve a more beautiful life.

821. Life is more beautiful if we have one or more true friends.

822. We can make our life more beautiful if we are organized.

823. Sociable individuals have much greater opportunities to achieve a beautiful life.

824. We can make life a lot more beautiful if we only act with an effective positive behavior.

825. Compliance with principles helps us achieve a beautiful life.

826. Life is more beautiful when you have successes.

827. A responsible behavior helps us have more opportunities to achieve a beautiful life.

828. If we use the Internet to the maximum in solving the problems and needs that we have, it would make our life much easier, more enjoyable, more beautiful. Good luck. If you have not connected yet, connect because it is worth it. Good luck.

829. We can make our life more beautiful if we plan our action very well.

830. Life is too beautiful to spend part of its freedom in prison to satisfy the desire of luxury.

831. The harmony between family members makes life more beautiful.

832. Life is too beautiful for a part of it to be spent in prison for negligence or lack of attention.

833. Regardless of how we live, it is not worth it to be alone which makes our life less beautiful.

834. Life has been given to us not to fight with it but to live it beautifully.

835. Hopes make our life more beautiful.

836. Activism makes our life more beautiful.

837. We can create a more beautiful life if we are less stressed.

838. We can create a more beautiful life if we are optimistic.

839. Life is too beautiful for us to spend a significant part of it in prison.

840. Co-development makes our life more beautiful.

841. Consensus helps us prevent and eliminate many obstacles in front of us on the road to achieving a more beautiful life.

842. We can make our life more beautiful if we are not stressed.

843. We can make life a lot more beautiful if we only have effective positive behaviors.

844. Life is more beautiful when we have successes.

845. A responsible behavior helps us have more chances to make our life more beautiful.

846. If we use the Internet to the maximum in solving problems and needs that we have, it makes our life easier, more enjoyable, more beautiful. Good luck. If you are not connected, connect as it is worth it for all reasons and purposes. Good luck.

847. A positive experience makes our life more beautiful.

848. Good humor makes our life more beautiful.

849. True friendship makes our life more beautiful.

850. Life would be much more beautiful without vices.

851.   Meditations help us make a more beautiful life.

852.   Most of the times social relations make life more beautiful.

853.   Friendships help us make a more beautiful life.

854.   The desire to lead a beautiful life must be owned by each of us.

855.   For people in the world's states there are much more chances and possibilities to obtain a more beautiful life with the help of technology.

856.   Life is much more beautiful when we have hopes.

857.   We can make life more beautiful if we have an appropriate education for us to achieve it.

858.   A psychological balance helps us make our life more beautiful.

859.   The capacity to take rapid decisions increases our possibilities to achieve a more beautiful life.

860.   Optimism helps us increase our chances of achieving a more beautiful live.

861.   Responsible people have much more chances to achieve a beautiful life.

862. An imaginative man has more chances to achieve a more beautiful life.

863. A man who is ready at any time to help somebody has greater chances of achieving a more beautiful life.

864. Those who know and have the power to change their inefficient behaviors when necessary have greater chances of achieving a more beautiful life.

865. A disciplined man has a greater potential to achieve a more beautiful life.

866. A complete compatibility of training with objectives helps us achieve a more beautiful life.

867. Financial independence helps us a lot in creating a more beautiful life.

868. Those who really love people have more chances to achieve a more beautiful life.

869. Very sociable and open persons will also achieve a more beautiful life.

870. Continuous, day by day self perfecting for as long as we live helps us achieve a more beautiful life.

871. Responsible men often succeed to achieve a beautiful life.

872. An energetic man has more chances to achieve a more beautiful life.

873. A man open towards new ideas has much more chances and a higher potential to achieve a more beautiful life.

874. An efficient communication helps a lot to achieve a more beautiful life.

875. People who succeed in carrying out the activities they had started have the capacity to achieve a more beautiful life.

876. Very sociable people have greater chances to achieve a more beautiful life.

877. Optimism makes our life a lot more beautiful.

878. The efficient management of our time helps us and increases our chances to achieve a beautiful life.

879. We need to use our life experience to achieve a more beautiful life.

880. Day by day the chances for more people to achieve a more beautiful life grow.

881. Credibility helps us a lot to make our life more beautiful.

882. Life can be more beautiful if we do not hate.

883. Life can be more beautiful if we do not hold grudges.

884. Humanist global thinking can create more possibilities for a higher number of people to achieve a more beautiful life.

885. People who produce useful ideas have bigger chances to achieve a more beautiful life.

886. A man who is emotionally stable has more chances to achieve a more beautiful life.

887. Self-imposed discipline helps us and contributes a lot in achieving a more beautiful life.

888. Those who prefer unstoppable positive activism have potential and great chances to achieve a beautiful life.

889. People with prejudice may not have a more beautiful life because of some prejudices.

890. People with wrong ideas may not achieve a more beautiful life because of wrong ideas.

891. An uncertainty of incomes makes achieving a more beautiful life more difficult.

892. People who know how to motivate other people have a bigger capacity to achieve a more beautiful life.

893. The right partner for life makes our life more beautiful.

894. Today, we have many chances of achieving a more beautiful life due to the Internet, the mobile, the development of information technologies, and the knowledge gained in all areas of activity.

895. Many of us can make life more beautiful than we think we can.

896. We must teach people how to make a more beautiful life because many of them do not know how although they want to.

897. Life can be beautiful and it is not worth consuming it with small things.

898. Experience increases our chances of making a beautiful life.

899. Those who are willing to try new paths have more and greater chances to achieve a beautiful life.

900. People with the sense of discipline have a higher capacity to achieve a more beautiful life.

901. Those who find unique ways to work effectively for a better life increase their possibilities to achieve a more beautiful life.

902. Those who have had better economic and social conditions during their evolution usually have a higher capacity to achieve a more beautiful life.

903. The state of nervosity stops us from achieving a more beautiful life.

904. Humanist ideas help us achieve a more beautiful life.

905. Skilled people have more and greater chances to achieve a more beautiful life.

906. People who are full of life and active have greater and more chances to achieve a more beautiful life.

907. People who are not careful with others achieve a beautiful life a lot harder.

908. The sense of quality increases our needs to achieve a more beautiful life.

909. The sense of fairness increases our chances to achieve a more beautiful life.

910. People who inspire trust have more abilities to achieve a more beautiful life.

911. Those who solve problems only through constructive methods have greater chances of achieving a more beautiful life.

912.	It is certain that our life can be much more beautiful if we give the necessary attention and time to achieving and maintaining a beautiful life.

913.	Life is a lot more beautiful when we do not argue.

914.	The ability of learning how to learn increases our chances of achieving a more beautiful life.

915.	Orientation towards a goal increases our chances of achieving a more beautiful life.

916.	Openness towards the world increases our possibilities of achieving a more beautiful life.

917.	A man who is satisfied by his own social behavior has chances of achieving a beautiful life.

918.	A strategic vision increases our chances to achieve a more beautiful future.

919.	The ability of rapid perception helps us a lot to increase our chances to achieve a more beautiful life.

920.	New efficient ways of thinking increase our chances to achieve a more beautiful life.

921.	Those who love what they do very much will achieve a beautiful life.

922. Those who passionately live their life have great chances of achieving a very beautiful life.

923. The lack of neurotic symptoms contributes a lot in achieving a more beautiful life.

924. The quality of sensing situations helps us a lot to achieve a beautiful life.

925. Orientation towards a future world increases our chances of achieving a more beautiful life.

926. Past and present experiences contribute a lot in achieving a more beautiful life.

927. Confidence in ourselves helps us a lot to make our life more beautiful.

928. A man who acts continuously, day by day to become even more organized has more and greater chances to achieve a more beautiful life.

929. A full compatibility of training with the objectives helps us achieve a beautiful life.

930. Those who cherish their collaborators have a greater potential to achieve a more beautiful life.

931. Those who know how to efficiently plan their actions will succeed in achieving a more beautiful life.

932. True friendships help us a lot to more quickly and easily achieve a more beautiful life.

933. Our value system helps us and contributes to achieving a more beautiful life.

934. People who are resistant to stress have much more chances to achieve a more beautiful life.

935. A man who cooperates in activities has much more chances to achieve a more beautiful life.

936. A trust-worthy a man has the potential to help him achieve a more beautiful life.

937. A man who approaches and is used to approach problems simultaneously from different points of view has much more chances and a greater potential to achieve a beautiful life.

938. The richness of existence helps us achieve a more beautiful life.

939. The man's need to achieve has contributed a lot to achieving many beautiful lives.

940. Those who have the sense of objectivity have more and greater chances to achieve a more beautiful life.

941.	Those who have opportunities to develop have much more and greater chances to achieve a more beautiful life.

942.	Life is a lot more beautiful when you love and you are loved by the person you love.

943.	Positive ideas make our life a lot more beautiful.

944.	Life is more beautiful when you have friends.

945.	Friendships make our life more beautiful.

946.	Efficient friendships can help us make a more beautiful life.

947.	When we are optimistic we can feel life more beautiful.

948.	Life is a lot more beautiful when you have true friendships.

949.	A life without arguments is a lot more beautiful.

950.	Life is a lot more beautiful when you feel you truly live it.

951.	Man's most beautiful ideal is that of achieving a true reciprocal love.

952.	Life with an optimistic husband is more beautiful.

Behavior

953.   Behavior for luxury can be prevented by positive thinking.

954.   Selflessness is a model of positive behavior that is necessary to appreciate.

955.   We can prevent conceit by self-controlling our behavior.

956.   Haughty behavior is very harmful to us.

957.   Haughty behavior creates a distance for many people.

958.   To envy others is a negative behavior.

959.   Positive behaviors lead us to happiness.

960.   The self-control of our behaviors can lead us to greater or smaller successes.

961.   The more idols we have the more necessary it is that all our behaviors be positive.

962.   All the educational institutions in the world need to form and develop unselfish thinking and selfless behavior.

963.   Impatience is a behavior that can sometimes create very large disasters. For this reason it is necessary to prevent becoming impatient in inappropriate situations.

964. Envy is an incorrect behavior that damages us, and sometimes it can cause us enormously much damage.

965. Enmities are incorrect behaviors that damage, sometimes, both us, as well as those who are our enemies.

966. In life it is necessary and good to have behaviors that do not bring us enemies.

967. In any situation, no matter how difficult it would be, it is necessary to have a responsible behavior.

968. Sometimes, our hastiness makes us make very big mistakes, with large negative effects, both for us and for others. So, beware, let us always avoid hastily behavior.

969. Flexibility in thinking and behavior helps us achieve much easier, much faster and a larger number of personal goals.

970. Shrewish behavior can be prevented.

971. Brutality is a negative behavior that we can prevent.

972. Greed is a negative behavior that is necessary to prevent.

973. Unfortunately, society is not concerned enough, does not take the necessary measures to prevent the causes that lead

certain people in a position where they need social protection and ensure the needed and obligatory human protection for people who need it.

974.   In fact, through this inhuman, ineffective, irresponsible, illegal, selfish, abusive, etc. behavior, society, unfortunately, has a great contribution to the achievement of many crimes committed by people who needed human protection and were not given any.

975.   The continuous return of any harmful behavior for us is one of the factors that make us happy a lot of times.

976.   Where necessary, it is good to change attitudes and behavior because only so we can achieve happiness.

977.   Those who have successes, have some specific behaviors that make them achieve success. From these people, it is necessary to take things by observing these behaviors that lead to success.

978.   Abstention is a quality, a behavior that is necessary for both spouses to have because abstention in situations that require the prevention of conflicts, they worsen the negative conflicts, quarrels, misunderstandings, disputes of marriage and sometimes even marriage itself.

979.   Goodness is a quality and a positive
        behavior that each of us needs to have, but
        unfortunately there are still many people
        who have no kindness.

980.   The capacity and art to foresee can be
        formed and developed every day by
        practicing through forethought behaviors
        specific to our daily situation.

981.   Selfish behavior should be replaced with
        ego altruist behavior in most cases.

982.   Ego altruist behavior is a behavior that takes
        into account both the interests of the
        personal self, and those of others, acting to
        satisfy both, for a harmonious cohabitation
        for itself and for the other.

983.   For those who have many great successes
        we can always learn more effective
        behaviors that may lead us and to many and
        great successes.

984.   He who is insidious in his behavior alienates
        people.

985.   By studying how they manage time, those
        people who have had many and great
        successes can help us learn more effective
        behaviors than ours.

986.   Our conflicting behavior makes people avoid
        cooperating with us.

987. Those who have conflicting behavior can eliminate it by the self-control of their behavior.

988. Harmful behaviors can be prevented through self-control, through the values that we have, through will and by establishing personal goals to prevent harmful behaviors for us.

989. Positive behaviors are part of the previous happiness of many people.

990. As we have more experience in a field of activity, we have more courage in actions and behaviors, projects we have in areas that we want to achieve them in.

991. Routine and daily habits should not be a brake for us, an impassable barrier in the form of our other more efficient, more orderly, faster, etc. behaviors.

992. Those who fail to escape the routine of everyday habits have inefficient behavior, are messy, slow, chaotic, etc. and they will have many failures and few and small achievements in life.

993. People who have a great capacity to take the needs of achieving personal goals, learn and take the behavior more efficient, more orderly, faster, etc.; they will make life a lot more or less successful, will have many

joys, much satisfaction and happiness and will do what they want in life.

994.   If we somehow have inhumane behavior it is necessary to change immediately to human behavior.

995.   Effective behaviors help us expand opportunities to achieve positive personal goals.

996.   Weariness can be prevented through proper diet, education, positive behavior balanced intellectual exercise, perseverance, will, exercise, a value system that we believe in and that we respect, business dynamism, social relations, friends, mature love, a happy marriage, adequate rest when necessary, appropriate sleep, entertainment, etc.

997.   Selfish behavior should be replaced with egoaltruist behavior in most cases.

998.   Egoaltruist behavior is a behavior that takes into account both the interests of the personal self, and those of others, acting to satisfy both, for a harmonious cohabitation for itself and for the other.

999.   Incorrect behavior of the husband towards his wife leads to decreased confidence of the wife in the husband.

1000.   The correct behavior of a husband towards his wife leads to increased confidence in him by his wife.

1001.   Men who are aggressive against a family member may change in behavior. Those who say they can not change in behavior and they will not be aggressive towards one of the members of his family are wrong.

1002.   The respect of the wife towards the husband is achieved through a positive behavior of her husband towards her and the other members of his family.

1003.   We need to have the caution that it is necessary today to form and cultivate a cautious behavior.

1004.   When employees are wrong, leaders need to have normal reactions, a normal responsible behavior, and to consider that the employee who made a mistake and causes mistakes should take the necessary steps to prevent other mistakes that may be made by the employee who made a mistake and by other employees.

1005.   Enthusiastic behavior greatly increases our opportunities to achieve personal goals.

1006.   The men thanked for their social behavior are likely to become more credible.

1007. Those who know and have the power to change inefficient behaviors when it is necessary have greater chances to achieve efficient co operations.

1008. Our hostile non aggressive behavior helps us become more operative.

1009. The two spouses need to take very great care of each other, care for their individual behaviors so that they do not affect mature love.

1010. The judge must model positive behavior both in the courtroom and outside both at work and outside work.

1011. Verbal aggression in the family is a behavior that harms the family's happiness.

1012. As we have more successful friends, the more opportunities we have to take from them effective patterns of behavior.

1013. If you have any negative behavior it is necessary to change immediately to a positive behavior.

1014. Inefficient behaviors surely lead us to failures.

1015. Shallow inefficient behaviors must be terminated immediately and replaced with effective behaviors.

1016.   Inefficient behaviors put barriers in achieving our positive personal goals.

1017.   Effective behaviors help us have many more opportunities to meet favorable situations.

1018.   Successes can not be achieved without effective behavior.

1019.   For as long as we live we must seek to have relationships of friendship with special people, who have many successes, many qualities, many positive and effective behaviors in order to learn from them as much as possible. This rule, this principle helps us achieve much easier and more personal goals.

1020.   Incorrect behavior of the husband towards the wife leads to decreased confidence in her husband.

1021.   Correct behavior of the wife towards the husband leads to increased confidence in her husband.

1022.   In life we have more opportunities to meet favorable situations if we are friends with as many people who have had successes as possible, people which have qualities, skills, effective behaviors, creative qualities, which are well documented in the areas that concern us as well.

1023. Spouses have to agree on what they do in dealing with children, to have a unite behavior in order not to harm any children or relations between them.

1024. We can make life a lot more beautiful if we only act with an effective positive behavior.

1025. Recognizing and rewarding the positive behavior of children by their parents moves the children very much, making them continue in that positive behaviors.

1026. Some behaviors, such as a negative mentality, can lead to crimes.

1027. A responsible behavior helps us have more opportunities to achieve a beautiful life.

1028. We should always prevent suicidal behavior, attitudes, ideas and thoughts.

1029. The state is required to set up specialized services for the prevention and elimination of suicidal behaviors, attitudes, ideas and thoughts in order to reduce to a maximum the possibility of suicides.

1030. People want be respected but in many behaviors, unfortunately, they are thick-skinned.

1031. Senselessness is a much unappreciated behavior.

1032.   Each of us must reject rude behaviors.

1033.   Illiterate people as well as literate ones sometimes have behaviors that lack common sense.

1034.   Those who have common sense succeed to master it when people who have no common sense have behaviors that lack common sense.

1035.   Revenge is a preposterous behavior.

1036.   Revenge is a behavior of primitive debris.

1037.   Revenge is a primitive behavior.

1038.   Humanist thinking contributes greatly to maintaining a humane behavior in society.

1039.   Anger is an incorrect behavior with multiple negative effects.

1040.   Insulting is a primitive behavior.

1041.   Brutality is a primitive behavior.

1042.   Promptness is a very effective behavior.

1043.   Women who are aggressive against their family members may change their aggressive behavior to be a non-aggressive behavior in any family situation.

1044.   The correct behavior of a man towards his wife and other members of his family makes that man be very respected by his wife and members of his family.

1045.   Verbal aggression in the family is a primitive behavior.

1046.   Physical aggression in the family is a primitive behavior.

1047.   Each of us should have the power not to take negative patterns of behavior.

1048.   Tact is a behavior that helps us have many successes in life.

1049.   Cooperative behavior helps us have more opportunities to meet more favorable circumstances.

1050.   erbal aggression in a family is a behavior that damages the happiness of the family.

1051.   As we have more successful friends the more chances we have to take from them effective patterns of behavior.

1052.   Continuously, day by day, for as long as we live it is necessary to have the personal objective to prevent having negative behaviors.

1053.   If you have any negative behaviors you
         need to change them immediately with
         positive behaviors.

1054.   Inefficient behaviors surely lead us to failure.

1055.   Inefficient behaviors should be stopped
         immediately and replaced with effective
         behaviors.

1056.   Inefficient behaviors prevent us from
         achieving our positive personal objectives.

1057.   Effective behaviors help us have more
         chances to meet favorable situations.

1058.   Success can not be obtained without
         effective behaviors.

1059.   In life we have many more chances to meet
         favorable situations if we are friends with as
         many people as we can who have had
         successes, who have qualities, skills,
         effective behaviors, creative qualities, which
         are well documented in areas that concern
         us all.

1060.   Spouses need to agree in what there will be
         in their relationships with children, to have
         an equal behavior in order not to damage
         any children or relations between them.

1061.   We can make life a lot more beautiful if we
         only have effective positive behaviors.

1062. The recognition and rewarding of positive behaviors of children by parents motivate a lot of children, making them continue with those principles of positive behavior.

1063. Some behaviors, called mentalities, are not in fact mentalities, but crimes.

1064. A responsible behavior helps us have more chances to make our life more beautiful.

1065. We always need to prevent suicidal behavior, attitudes, ideas and suicidal thoughts.

1066. It is needed to establish specialized services for the prevention and elimination of suicidal behaviors, attitudes, ideas and thoughts to reduce to a maximum possible suicides.

1067. Negative behaviors must be immediately stopped and replaced with positive ones.

1068. A responsible behavior helps us have more chances of achieving efficient co operations.

1069. An aggressive behavior of the husband towards the wife is very harmful for children.

1070. Day by day it is necessary to have as an objective the removal of discriminatory behaviors.

1071. Discriminatory behavior is illegal and has very large negative effects.

1072. Discriminatory behaviors must be replaced with non-discriminative ones.

1073. Hatred is a primitive behavior.

1074. Not caring about the problems that regard us is an unfit behavior for a citizen.

1075. If we somehow have any inhumane behavior it is necessary to change to human behavior immediately.

1076. Effective behaviors help us increase our

1077. Those who know and have the power to change their inefficient behaviors when necessary have greater chances of achieving a more beautiful life.

1078. A non-hostile but aggressive behavior increases our potential of achieving personal goals.

1079. Those who have wise friends can learn many positive efficient behaviors.

1080. Those who have co operations with wise men can learn a lot from their efficient positive behaviors.

1081. An enthusiastic behavior increases our chances to realize effective co operations.

1082. Those who know and have the power to change their inefficient behaviors when necessary have great chances to achieve a true mature love.

1083. A non-hostile but aggressive behavior helps us a lot to become more efficient.

1084. Our behaviors must always be humane.

1085. Responsible behaviors must be promoted, supported and rewarded.

1086. Unfortunately, some televisions promote very harmful negatives models of behavior.

1087. Studying day by day, continuously we live the life of people around us, of those who have successes, and we have great possibilities to find more effective, positive behaviors that can help us a lot in achieving personal goals.

1088. Each of us needs to prevent irresponsible behaviors as they are very harmful both to us and to other persons.

1089. Irresponsible behaviors need to always be prevented because, unfortunately, although they are very harmful in many situations we often find them in 2007.

1090. Irresponsible behaviors very much reduce our credibility.

1091. Positive behaviors make us more credible.

1092. Humanist behaviors make us more credible.

1093. Mental behaviors make us more credible.

1094. Selfishness is one of the behaviors that stop the solving of many human problems.

1095. Selfishness is one of the behaviors that stop the achievement of efficient co operations.

1096. Envy is one of the negative behaviors that stop the achievement of true friendships.

1097. Meanness is one of the negative behaviors that stop the achievement of some efficient co operations.

1098. Anger is a primitive very harmful behavior.

1099. Continuously, day by day, for as long as we live it is necessary to prevent having negative behaviors because these behaviors can sometimes produce more or less harm.

1100. Enthusiastic behaviors make us more confident in success.

1101. Those who know and have the power to change their inefficient behaviors when necessary have great chances to meet the right partner for life.

1102. A non-hostile but aggressive behavior helps us a lot in achieving outstanding performances.

1103. Each of us needs to learn how to change our behaviors.

1104. A behavior oriented towards luxury is a primitive behavior.

1105. A behavioral oriented towards gambling is a behavior of despising the workplace.

1106. A behavior oriented towards luxury is a behavior that despises man.

1107. A wasteful behavior is a very harmful behavior both in society and for the one who wastes.

1108. People who have success have a very dynamic behavior.

1109. The majority of people who have successes have a corresponding behavior with others.

1110. The ability to form, develop and maintain only positive behaviors needs to be completed by the sense of responsibility.

1111. Studying day by day, continuously, for as long as we live, the life of people around us, of those who have successes, we have great possibilities of finding many efficient positive behaviors that can help us a lot in achieving our personal goals.

1112. Unfortunately, in 2007, there still are irresponsible behaviors of many people that negatively affect other people more or less. It is necessary and mandatory that all of these illegal behaviors are punished with tickets corresponding to their gravity and that they pay the damages and moral or psychical sufferings created in order to prevent repeating other irresponsible behaviors.

1113. Egoism is one of the behaviors that very much stop the achievement of efficient co-developments.

1114. In extremes, when a marriage can no longer continue and when it reaches a divorce, it is fair and necessary that the divorce is done in a friendly way, without meanness, reproaches, revenge, because negative behaviors harm both parties a lot and if there are children involved, because for children such a breakup is enormously harmful.

1115. Relations and behaviors of spouses during the divorce need to be positive, understanding and even mutually supportive.

1116. Thanklessness is a primitive behavior.

1117. A tolerant behavior helps us a lot in achieving true friendships.

1118. Social behavior helps us achieve efficient co operations more easily.

1119. Team spirit is the behavior that helps us achieve more and greater successes.

1120. Hesitating behavior reduces the operability of the decisions that we take.

1121. Those who know and have the power to change their inefficient behaviors have great chances of achieving a happy life.

1122. A non hostile but aggressive behavior increases our chances and all our potential of achieving more and greater successes.

1123. People with human social behaviors need to have the sense of commitment in everything they do.

1124. Those who know and have the power to change their inefficient behaviors when it is necessary have great chances to achieve outstanding performances.

1125. A non hostile but aggressive behavior helps us increase our credibility.

1126. Enthusiastic behavior increases our chances to meet more favorable situations.

1127. A man who is satisfied by his own social behavior has great chances to meet favorable situations.

Brutal

1128.   Brutality between spouses has no place.

1129.   The brutality between spouses enormously harms the marriage.

1130.   He who is brutal can sometimes cause much harm to himself.

1131.   He who brutal is not accepted by most people.

1132.   The brutality between spouses can be prevented.

Calm

1133.   Calm people in any situation have more chances to meet more favorable situations.

1134.   People who are calm in any situation have more chances to maintain a happy marriage.

1135.   The majority of people who have successes are calm in stressing situations.

1136.   People who do not have hopes of creating other groups need to connect with people who are calm in stressing situations.

1137.   Calm people in any situation have great chances of achieving efficient co operations.

1138.   People who are calm in any situation have more chances of achieving mature love.

1139.   A responsible man is also a calm man in any situation.

1140.   People who are calm in any situation have many chances to prevent many conflicts.

1141.   The prevention of stress can be achieved also through the contribution of the formation, development, maintenance and usage of calm behavior.

1142.   In order to trace and transform our personal objectives into reality it is necessary to form, develop, maintain and use the ability to be calm in any stressing situation.

1143.   A radical transformation for the better of our life can be achieved also through the contribution of the formation, development, maintenance and usage of the ability to be calm in any stressing situation.

1144.   In order to pursue and transform our personal goals into reality we need to form, develop, maintain and use the ability to be calm in any stressing situation.

1145.   Aspiring towards a more meaningful life can be achieved also through the contribution of the formation, development, maintenance and usage of the ability to be calm in any stressing situation.

1146.   We can prevent some failures also through the contribution of the formation, development, maintenance and usage of calm behaviors.

1147.   In order to pursue and transform our personal goals into reality we need to form and develop the ability to be calm in stressing situations.

1148.   Preventing stress can be achieved also through the contribution of the formation, development, maintenance and usage of calm behaviors.

1149.   Positive experience can be achieved also through the contribution of the formation, development and maintenance of the ability to be calm in stressing situations.

1150.   In order to pursue and transform our personal goals into reality we need to form, develop, maintain and use the ability to be calm in stressing situations.

1151.   Emancipation from restrictions can be made through the formation, development and maintenance of the ability to be calm in any situation.

1152.   Obtaining as many and greatest successes as we can, can be achieved through the formation, development and maintenance of the ability to be calm in any situation.

1153.   We can achieve our personal goals also through the formation, development, maintenance and usage of the ability to be calm in any situation.

1154.   Our own personality can be maintained through the ability to be calm in any stressing situation.

1155.   People who are calm in any situation are more credible.

1156.   Calm people prevent more trouble in all situations.

1157.   In order to prevent failures it is necessary to also form, develop, maintain and use calm behavior.

1158.   Problems cannot be solved by the ideas that created them but also through the contribution of the formation, development, maintenance and usage of calm behavior.

1159.   Some mistakes can be prevented also through the contribution of the formation, development, maintenance and usage of calm behavior.

1160.   Self-imposed discipline helps us become
        calm.

1161.   Release from our self-imposed restrictions
        can be made also through the contribution of
        the formation, development, maintenance
        and usage of calm behavior.

1162.   Rather than lamenting that we do not have
        successes it is more useful to also form,
        develop, maintain and use calm behavior.

1163.   Our future can be projected and achieved
        also through the contribution of the
        formation, development, maintenance and
        usage of calm behavior.

1164.   Continuous self-motivation helps us become
        calm.

1165.   In order to escape poverty it is necessary to
        also form, develop, maintain and use calm
        behavior.

1166.   We can form, develop and maintain the
        state of being ourselves also through the
        contribution of the formation, development,
        maintenance and usage of a calm behavior.

1167.   We can prevent some failures also through
        the contribution of the formation,
        development, maintenance and usage of
        calm behavior.

Careful

1168.   Those with the sense of efficiency are more careful.

1169.   Careful people must be rewarded.

1170.   Careful people have greater chances to maintain mature love.

1171.   Sometimes our so-called true friends can get us in the biggest troubles possible, can sleep with our wife or with our husband, with our girlfriend or boyfriend, can take away our business, etc. Look around you. Be very careful for the so called true friendship.

1172.   True friendship is formed and maintained very difficultly and can break in a second. So be very careful. Do not play with it.

1173.   We can prevent negative actions if we are more careful in what we do.

1174.   Parents should be very careful with children and never forget to recognize all their positive achievements, to reward them in one way or another.

1175.   We can make our life more beautiful if we are always careful.

1176.   Illegal actions can destroy mature, true love. Is it worth it? No. So be careful.

1177.   Be careful in life at what is worth and not worth doing.

1178.   The states' institutions need to manage the public money more carefully, more efficiently, more responsibility because now this leaves much to be desired.

1179.   Parents need to be very careful with children and never forget to recognize their positive achievements, to reward them in one way or another.

1180.   Fear makes us be more careful.

1181.   Human mind is diabolical, it can achieve positive incredible facts, but unfortunately also facts that may be enormously, incredibly negative. So be careful, a man can do what an angel can, but at the same time he can do what the devil can too.

1182.   Careful people must be appreciated.

1183.   Careful people have more and greater chances to achieve more and greater successes.

1184.   People who are in love are sometimes less careful.

1185.   We need to be permanently careful at how we order and reorder our priorities of personal goals.

1186. People who are careful must be supported.

1187. Young people need and must be very careful not to make the same mistakes as their predecessors by taking from their experience only positive models and experience

1188. Careful men have fewer failures.

1189. People who are careful must be promoted.

1190. People who are careful have greater and more chances to achieve personal goals.

1191. By listening very carefully to what people who have had successes say and by taking from them the ideas that are useful we can form, develop, maintain and use a positive live conception.

1192. By listening very carefully to what people who have had successes say and by taking from them the ideas that are useful to us we can form, develop, maintain and use the ideas that help us motivate ourselves.

1193. People who are not careful with others are not rewarded.

1194. By listening very carefully to what successful people say we only have to gain.

1195.   AGC mediations help us are just meditate
        more and more carefully the problems we
        have to solve.

1196.   Our chances of becoming happy increase if
        we are careful.

1197.   Continuously making ourselves efficient
        helps us become careful.

1198.   Continuous self perfection helps us become
        careful.

1199.   Life would have much less trouble if we
        would be more careful in every action of
        ours.

1200.   We can prevent many unpleasant surprises
        if we are also sufficiently careful in
        everything we do and think.

1201.   Greed has led many people to bankruptcy,
        so be very carefully and prevent getting
        greedy.

Cheerful

1202.   Cheerful people have chances to gather
        around them other people who are also in a
        good mood.

1203.   People who are in love are usually more
        cheerful.

1204.   In order to follow and transform our personal goals into reality, it is necessary to also form, develop, maintain and use our cheerful behavior.

1205.   Pessimism can be removed and replaced with optimism also through the contribution of the formation, development, maintenance and usage of cheerful behavior.

1206.   Problems cannot be solved by the ideas that created them but also through the contribution of the formation, development, maintenance and usage of cheerful behavior.

1207.   Our resistance to changing for the better can be overcome also through the contribution of the formation, development, maintenance and usage of cheerful behavior.

1208.   The self efficient use of our time helps us become cheerful.

1209.   In order to prevent not achieving our personal goals, it is necessary to also form, develop, maintain and use our cheerful behavior.

1210.   Creativity helps us become cheerful.

1211.   In order to escape poverty it is necessary to also form, develop, maintain and use cheerful behavior.

1212. Stress can be prevented also through the formation, development, maintenance and usage of cheerful behavior.

1213. We can contribute to the achievement of our greatest accomplishments also through the contribution of the formation, development, maintenance and usage of cheerful behavior.

1214. The force of our ideas can be augmented also through the contribution of the formation, development, maintenance and usage of cheerful behavior.

1215. The radical transformation for the better of our life can be achieved also through the formation, development, maintenance and usage of cheerful behavior.

1216. Our future can be projected and achieved also through the contribution of the formation, development, maintenance and usage of cheerful behavior.

1217. Continuously making ourselves efficient helps us become cheerful.

1218. Hope helps us become cheerful.

1219. In order to rise up once again for the first time for the who knows what time it is necessary to also form, develop, maintain and use cheerful behavior.

1220. In achieving our successes a contribution is also brought by the formation, development, maintenance and usage of cheerful behavior.

1221. The limits of achievement imposed by ourselves in our mind at a given moment can be overcome or eliminated also through the contribution of the formation, development, maintenance and usage of cheerful behavior.

1222. Release from our self-imposed restrictions can be made also through the contribution of the formation, development, maintenance and usage of cheerful behavior.

1223. Wisdom helps us become cheerful.

1224. The solutions to the problems we have or that we want to solve can be found also through the contribution of the formation, development, maintenance and usage of cheerful behavior.

1225. Continuous self-motivation helps us become cheerful.

1226. Responsibility helps us become cheerful.

1227. Will helps us become cheerful.

1228. Rather than lamenting that we do not have successes it is more useful to also form, develop, maintain and use cheerful behavior.

1229.   Acting efficiently helps us become cheerful.

1230.   The necessary qualities in achieving personal goals can be formed, developed, maintained and used also through the contribution of the formation, development, maintenance and usage of cheerful behavior.

1231.   We can prevent some failures also through the contribution of the formation, development, maintenance and usage of cheerful behavior.

1232.   Aspiring towards a more meaningful life can also be achieved through the formation, development, maintenance and usage of cheerful behavior.

1233.   Our own happiness can be achieved and maintained also through the contribution of the formation, development, maintenance and usage of cheerful behavior.

1234.   Continuous self perfection helps us become cheerful.

1235.   In order to prevent failures it is necessary to also form, develop, maintain and use cheerful behavior.

1236.   The obstacles that prevent us from achieving our personal goals can be surpassed also through the contribution of the formation, development, maintenance and usage of cheerful behavior.

1237.   Some mistakes can be prevented also through the contribution of the formation, development, maintenance and usage of cheerful behavior.

1238.   Optimism helps us become cheerful.

1239.   Positive experience can be achieved also through the contribution of the formation, development, maintenance and usage of cheerful behavior.

1240.   Communication helps us become cheerful.

1241.   We can become stronger and we can not allow ourselves to be influenced by the world also through the contribution of the formation, development, maintenance and usage of cheerful behavior.

1242.   Self-imposed discipline helps us become cheerful.

1243.   We can overcome the difficulties that we must overcome also through the help of the formation, development, maintenance and usage of cheerful behavior.

1244. Our happiness depends a lot also on the formation, development, maintenance and usage of cheerful behavior.

1245. Confidence in ourselves helps us become cheerful.

1246. Cherishing oneself helps us become cheerful.

1247. We can prevent the falling apart of a happy marriage also through the contribution of the formation, development, maintenance and usage of cheerful behavior.

1248. Continuous self-control helps us become cheerful.

1249. Obtaining more and greater successes can be achieved also through the contribution of the formation, development, maintenance, usage of a cheerful behavior.

1250. Hopes can be created also through the contribution of the formation, development, maintenance and usage of cheerful behavior.

1251. We can form, develop and maintain the state of being ourselves also through the contribution of the formation, development, maintenance and usage of a cheerful behavior.

Comfort

1252. An unsatisfied need creates psychological discomfort.

1253. Through marriage a woman tries to resolve her need for safety and to achieve a certain psychological comfort.

1254. The need for safety and psychological comfort, a woman can only achieve through cooperation with her husband.

1255. Good humor is a state of optimal psychological comfort.

1256. Those who do not persevere in life, have less opportunities to achieve personal goals. Do not be comfortable, you'll persevere and succeed. Good luck.

1257. Marriage should provide psychological comfort to its members.

1258. The psychological discomfort of the family should be prevented.

1259. The psychological discomfort caused by marriage is very damaging to that marriage and the affected ones.

1260. A family is necessary to have harmonious mutual relations, so that each has a part of psychological comfort in the family.

1261.   Prolonged mental discomfort harms our health very much.

1262.   The psychological discomfort generated in the family very much affects the work.

1263.   Psychological discomfort greatly decreases the effectiveness of creative abilities.

1264.   Verbal aggression in the family leads to the creation of psychological discomfort in the family.

1265.   The psychological comfort of the family helps greatly to the achievement of personal goals.

1266.   The state of psychical discomfort can be removed through the formation, development and support of creative thinking.

1267.   I can feel a strong psychical discomfort when I see injustices done to people.

1268.   Friendships create a special psychical comfort.

1269.   The comforting of lovers brings them very close.

1270.   The comforting of lovers increases their mutual sexual attraction.

1271. The comforting of lovers contributes a lot to maintaining true love.

1272. The comforting of spouses contributes a lot to maintaining a happy marriage.

1273. Lovers can increase their sexual appetite also through comforting.

1274. Spouses can maintain their sexual appetite also through comforting.

1275. Lovers can maintain their sexual desire also through comforting.

1276. Comforting must be rewarded with comforting.

1277. By talking about our own emotions we create a state of psychical comfort.

1278. Argumentative talks create psychical discomfort.

1279. Loyalty creates psychical comfort.

1280. Caresses between lovers also create psychical comfort.

1281. Caresses between spouses also create psychical comfort.

1282. Life is much more beautiful in a marriage when caresses and comforting exists between the two spouses.

Communication

1283. Efficient communication is also realized with the help of the exchange of information.

1284. Human communication greatly increases the chances to achieve personal goals.

1285. Human communication helps us keep our marriage happy.

1286. The Internet is an ideal place to facilitate communication and human contact 24 hours a day and it is the most convenient, less costly at any time of day and night way, with a great number of people. Connect to the Internet if you have not connected yet because it is worth doing it. Good luck.

1287. Achieving a happy marriage is not done by itself, but through many efforts, much dedication, a lot of tolerance, more rational compromises, mutual trust between spouses, a lot of communication, much mutual respect, a lot of knowledge, a lot of wisdom on both sides, much fairness, etc.

1288. Human communication greatly increases our chances to achieve personal goals.

1289. The Internet is ideal as it facilitates and enhances human communication 24 hours a day any day and with the most convenient, low cost at any time of day and night, with an unlimited number of people. Connect to the Internet if you have not signed in yet, because it is worth it. Good luck.

1290. Communication increases our chances of achieving efficient co operations.

1291. The Internet, telephone, media communications contribute to developing and promoting co-development thinking.

1292. An efficient communication increases our chances of meeting favorable situations.

1293. Human communication greatly increases our chances to keep our efficient co-development.

1294. Without an efficient human communication no efficient cooperation can be achieved.

1295. The exchange of information contributes a lot to achieving an efficient human communication.

1296. An efficient communication helps us a lot to succeed in life.

1297. The exchange of information helps achieve an efficient communication.

1298. Efficient communication helps us a lot in global humanization.

1299.   The technology of information and communications will be the technology of the future.

1300.   Positive ideas who can change people's life for the better need to be promoted continuously, day by day, on the Internet and through other technologies of communications.

1301.   Efficient human communication is the key of many successes.

1302.   Efficient human communication contributes a lot in achieving more and greater successes.

1303.   Human communication is good for our health.

1304.   Those who have efficient communication have more chances to succeed in life.

1305.   Efficient communication contributes a lot to maintaining social relations.

1306.   Efficient communication contributes a lot to achieving true friendships.

1307.   Positive ideas who can change people's life for the better need to be promoted continuously, day by day, on the Internet and through other technologies of communications.

1308.   Efficient human communication is the key of
        many successes.

1309.   Efficient human communication contributes
        a lot in achieving more and greater
        successes.

1310.   Human communication is good for our
        health.

1311.   Those who have efficient communication
        have more chances to succeed in life.

Concern

1312.   Most of us do not have as a permanent
        objective the achievement of a good life and
        we are not even seriously concerned to
        reach it. So how can we have a beautiful
        life?

1313.   Life for many of us can be more beautiful if
        we are concerned with making it more
        beautiful.

1314.   Unfortunately, neither people nor society
        address the future, are not concerned with
        the future that is so important to us, with
        how much it influences our future happiness.

1315.   In most people's concerns regarding their
        objectives, their projects in different future
        aspects virtually do not exist neither in
        theoretical approaches nor do they speak

about plans, projects, targets achieved. This fact makes their life one lived largely at random from hand to mouth, as many are not happy in the future ahead.

1316.   I am not saying that women should not be concerned with their outer beauty but to occupy themselves more with their inner beauty, to achieve and maintain a happy marriage. For these targets women fortunately have unlimited capacities but unfortunately very few use them.

1317.   Unfortunately, society is not concerned enough, does not take the necessary measures to prevent the causes that lead certain people in a position where they need social protection and ensure the needed and obligatory human protection for people who need it.

1318.   In fact, through this inhuman, ineffective, irresponsible, illegal, selfish, abusive, etc. behavior, society, unfortunately, has a great contribution to the achievement of many crimes committed by people who needed human protection and were not given any.

1319.   True friends can help us enormously to achieve our happiness and we, in turn, help them achieve theirs. We can much easier make both new and true friends as our objectives to help us become happy. This makes us have a special care and concern, with much dedication to form, develop and maintain relations of true friends and mutual activities, common actions, etc..

1320.   In 2007, in most people in the world most behaviors are selfish behaviors unfortunately, they are very harmful ones because such behaviors are concerned with in particular, the interests of their own persons, irrespective of the fact that they often harm other people and in some exceptional cases people even die, or have huge damages.

1321.   People who are always concerned about the future also have creative qualities.

1322.   Lack of insufficient jobs in some countries is primarily attributable to insufficient concern for sufficient job creation of those who have that obligation by law.

1323.   States should be concerned about citizens especially for an efficient education suitable to all intents and purposes that meet real needs of education of people and society so that both needs are effectively met.

1324.   Those who are concerned with creating an optimal cooperation in a team have humanist qualities.

1325.   In life we have more opportunities to meet favorable situations if we are friends with as many people who have had successes as possible, people which have qualities, skills, effective behaviors, creative qualities, which are well documented in the areas that concern us as well.

1326.   The excessive consumption of alcohol makes the people concerned have problems in achieving personal goals.

1327.   Conceit in a family harms the concerned family very much.

1328.   To make us more easily and quickly achieve our personal goals is to accumulate as much knowledge as possible about how to build the future in what concerns our personal goals.

1329.   Trade unions should be more concerned about finding jobs for those who have reduced employment for objective reasons.

1330.   States are not sufficiently concerned with the creation of work places.

1331.   States are not sufficiently concerned, in a necessary and effective way, with the prevention of the lack of compliance with the laws.

1332. In life we have many more chances to meet favorable situations if we are friends with as many people as we can who have had successes, who have qualities, skills, effective behaviors, creative qualities, which are well documented in areas that concern us all.

1333. Spouses need to be concerned with maintaining the unity and trust between them after they have children, so that children do not have their unity and trust affected.

1334. Meditations make us give more attention and time in all that concerns us.

1335. A psychological balance can be maintain once achieved through the proper nutrition of the person concerned, through education, intellectual work, perseverance, experience, willingness, physical exercises, etc.

1336. Positive thinking can be achieved if you do not have it through the proper nutrition of the person concerned, through education, intellectual work, perseverance, experience, willingness, physical exercises, etc.

1337. Good mood can be achieved if the person concerned has adequate nourishment, it can be achieved through education, intellectual work, perseverance, willpower, exercise, a value system that we believe in and that we respect, business dynamism, social relationships, friends, mature love and a happy marriage.

1338.   Fatigue can be prevented through the proper nutrition of the person concerned, through education, positive behavior, balanced life, intellectual exercises, perseverance, willpower, exercise, a value system that we believe in and that we respect, business dynamism, social relations, friends, mature love, a happy marriage, adequate rest when necessary, proper sleep, entertainment, etc..

1339.   States should be especially concerned to achieve a proper education effective from all points of view to respond to real the needs of education of the people and society and to effectively satisfy both their needs.

1340.   In 2007 the behaviors of the majority of people in the world are mostly selfish behaviors unfortunately. They are very harmful because these behaviors are particularly concerned with the interests of his own people, irrespective of the account that they damage other people and in some cases, exceptional people even die or huge damages are made.

1341.   The inner beauty of a woman, as long as the woman is concerned, contributes the most in achieving mature love.

1342. People who have had successes have succeeded in surpassing the states of concern.

1343. The inner beauty of a young man as far as the young man is concerned contributes to most in achieving mature love.

1344. Not being concerned about what others might think of us helps us achieve more pleasant surprises.

Conflict

1345. Conflict prevention is a necessity for every one of us.

1346. Non-discrimination prevents many conflicts.

1347. The one who is quick in anger creates many conflicts.

1348. One's self-control prevents many conflicts.

1349. Totalitarianism creates conflicts.

1350. Arrogance leads to many conflicts.

1351. Those with tact succeed in avoiding misunderstandings, conflicts, arguments, annoyances within the family.

1352. Both the wife and husband should not provoke jealousy to each other because this can harm them enormously much in certain situations, and even lead to divorce, to arguments and continuous conflict, unbearable tension which could lead to divorce.

1353.   When respect disappears between spouses in a family, disputes arise, conflicts, arguments, mistrust and ultimately it is very likely in many families for divorce to occur.

1354.   Each of the spouses need to always be calculated in family relations in order to prevent arguments, conflicts, misunderstandings etc..

1355.   The tact of each spouse enormously helps them prevent many conflicts, arguments, misunderstandings, dispute and even divorce.

1356.   Abstention is a quality, a behavior that is necessary for both spouses to have because abstention in situations that require the prevention of conflicts, they worsen the negative conflicts, quarrels, misunderstandings, disputes of marriage and sometimes even marriage itself.

1357.   Caution in marriage helps us enormously to avoid conflicts, arguments, hate, distrust and sometimes even divorce. The more each of the spouses is cautious the better it is.

1358.   Forethought is a quality that is required of each spouse in the family. Only with forethought a husband and wife can avoid many potential trouble, failures, conflicts, etc. in marriage.

1359.   Consensus is a situation that prevents many conflicts, trouble, divisive, arguments, loss of time etc..

1360.   Our conflicting behavior makes people avoid cooperating with us.

1361.   Those who have conflicting behavior can eliminate it by the self-control of their behavior.

1362.   Mental self-development is of enormous help in preventing a lot of failures, sorrows, mistakes, illnesses, accidents, conflicts, arguments, divorces, negative actions, inefficiencies, etc.

1363.   When we think constructively not destructively, we think this helps us prevent many mistakes, failures, accidents, divorces, misfortunes, conflicts, which are bad, harmful to us or others.

1364.   Those who have had a negative thinking in certain situations had many troubles, failures, conflicts in the family, some came to divorce, and they have achieved little success too.

1365.   Co-development prevents many conflicts.

1366.   Cooperation prevents many conflicts.

1367.   Responsibility prevents conflicts.

1368.   Common values prevent conflicts.

1369.   Self- control prevents many conflicts

1370.   Co-development thinking prevents conflict.

1371.   Respecting the right to nondiscrimination of people contributes a lot to preventing many conflicts.

1372.   People who have had successes have succeeded many times in solving conflicting situations.

1373.   Humanist economy would lead to preventing many international conflicts and wars.

1374.   Humanist economy can reduce sufferings, troubles, accidents, conflicts, negative effects of actions a lot.

1375.   Discipline prevents conflicts.

1376.   Efficient global co operations will prevent many possible conflicts.

1377.   Humanist global cooperation contributes a lot in reducing the number of armed and unarmed conflicts.

1378. The greater good prevents many conflicts.

1379. An agile man knows how to prevent conflicts.

1380. he quality of sensing situations helps us prevent conflicts.

1381. The quality of sensing situations helps us prevent conflicts.

1382. People who have everything know how to prevent many conflicts.

1383. Unresolved conflicts at the workplace lead to resignations, transfers, annulments of work contracts, etc.

1384. People who are calm in any situation have many chances to prevent many conflicts.

1385. A realistic man in interpersonal relations has greater chances to avoid many conflicts.

1386. Positive actions prevent many conflicts.

1387. Our responsibility helps us prevent many possible conflicts.

1388. People who are calm in any situation prevent many conflicts.

1389. Positive ideas prevent many potential conflicts.

1390. Common values help us a lot to prevent many conflicts.

1391. Positive imagination helps us prevent many conflicts.

1392. By preventing the formation of causes of conflicts we can prevent the apparition of conflicts.

1393. Conflicts can be prevented.

1394. Continuous conflicts are bad for our health.

1395. Conflicts can be avoided most of the times.

1396. Spouses must always avoid conflicting talks.

1397. Knowing ourselves helps us a lot to prevent many conflicts.

1398. A vigilant man has more chances to prevent more conflicts.

1399. The self-control of our behaviors helps us a lot to prevent some conflicts.

1400. Preventing conflicts helps us achieve more successes.

1401. The ability to solve conflicts helps us achieve more successes.

1402. Preventing conflicts helps us achieve more favorable chances.

Conscientious

1403. People who are conscientious at work are preferred in employment. So one of the keys to certainly obtain a job is to be conscientious at the workplace. Be aware that you will find a job if you are looking to find it. Do not let yourself beat by obstacles. Good luck. I'm with you.

1404. The man who is conscientious to positive influences achieves others in his life.

1405. Conscientiousness helps us a lot in achieving much more success.

1406. In achieving our successes a contribution is also brought by the formation, development, maintenance and usage of conscientious behavior.

1407. Our own happiness can be achieved and maintained also through the contribution of the formation, development, maintenance and usage of conscientious behavior.

1408. The necessary qualities in achieving personal goals can be formed, developed, maintained and used also through the contribution of the formation, development, maintenance and usage of conscientious behavior.

1409.	We can become stronger and we can not allow ourselves to be influenced by the world also through the contribution of the formation, development, maintenance and usage of conscientious behavior.

1410.	In order to prevent failures it is necessary to also form, develop, maintain and use conscientious behavior.

1411.	Continuous self-motivation helps us become conscientious.

1412.	Some mistakes can be prevented also through the contribution of the formation, development, maintenance and usage of conscientious behavior.

1413.	Our future can be projected and achieved also through the contribution of the formation, development, maintenance and usage of conscientious behavior.

1414.	In order to rise up once again for the first time for the who knows what time it is necessary to also form, develop, maintain and use conscientious behavior.

1415.	Release from our self-imposed restrictions can be made also through the contribution of the formation, development, maintenance and usage of conscientious behavior.

168

Conscious

1416. Those who are very conscious have a greater trust in themselves.

1417. Consciousness makes us even more efficient.

1418. A conscious man realizes his achievements especially based on his consciousness.

1419. Those who build their life on rational conscious bases achieve outstanding performances.

1420. Those who build their life on rational conscious bases have a higher potential to achieve happy marriages.

1421. A conscious man has a great potential to obtain more and higher successes in life.

1422. Those who build their lives on conscious rational bases have greater possibilities to achieve true friendships.

1423. He who is very conscious is much appreciated.

1424. He who is very conscious most of the time achieves his desired future.

1425. Those who are very conscious are the engines of progress in all fields of active

1426.   The ability to consciously choose makes us contribute more to achieving the greater good.

1427.   Most of those who have the ability to consciously choose have a great capacity to achieve efficient co-developments.

1428.   The possibility to consciously choose helps us achieve the desired social relations.

1429.   The ability to choose consciously increases our capacity of participating in efficient global co operations.

1430.   The majority of those who have the ability to consciously choose have the capacity to achieve a mature love.

1431.   The majority of those who have the ability to consciously choose develop their trust in the future.

1432.   Many people are unconscious and irresponsible and mock their happy marriage.

1433.   Consciousness helps us a lot to achieve a more beautiful life.

1434.   The ability to consciously choose makes us more efficient.

1435.   The ability to consciously choose helps us a lot to achieve our own happiness.

1436. Those who have the ability to consciously choose have a greater capacity to achieve more and greater successes.

1437. Those who have the ability to consciously choose have a greater capacity to achieve their personal goals.

1438. Most of those who have the ability to consciously choose have a greater capacity to achieve a more beautiful life.

1439. The ability to consciously choose helps us a lot to achieve our desired future.

1440. Those who have the ability to consciously choose must be appreciated.

1441. Most of those who have the obligation of consciously choosing have the ability to maintain a mature love.

1442. The majority of those who have the ability of consciously choosing have more and greater chances to meet more favorable situations.

1443. Most of those who have the ability to consciously choose have a greater capacity to become more performing.

1444. The ability to consciously choose is an engine of development in all areas of activity.

1445. The ability to consciously choose requires a great exchange of information.

1446. Most of those who have the ability to consciously choose have the ability to select a happy marriage.

1447. Most of those who have the capacity of consciously choosing prevent many mistakes.

1448. The ability to consciously choose increases our capacity to succeed in life.

1449. Consciousness helps us become more performant.

1450. Consciousness helps us achieve effective co operations.

Control

1451. One's self-control prevents us from much trouble.

1452. In any situation we find ourselves in, no matter how tough it is, we should avoid losing control.

1453. We can control greed if we want to.

1454. In any difficult situation, no matter how difficult it is, it is necessary not to lose our self control, our temper.

172

1455. Those who have conflicting behavior can eliminate it by the self-control of their behavior.

1456. Harmful behaviors can be prevented through self-control, through the values that we have, through will and by establishing personal goals to prevent harmful behaviors for us.

1457. Self-control helps us make true friends.

1458. The cases of the bankruptcies of firms are innumerable, some of which may be known that the company will go bankrupt, others come from external factors that can not be controlled generated by us, such as bankruptcy has unexpectedly unite customers and no one can collect money from them any more.

1459. Leaders need more than employees and companies to control their impulses, not to have exaggerated effects in certain situations.

1460. The man capable of self-control in stressful situations has the power to face any unpleasant surprises.

1461. A man with self control knows how to realize a more beautiful life.

1462. Those who have big preferences for positive uncontrollable activism contribute a lot to many exchanges of information.

1463. Those who have big preferences for positive uncontrollable activism have potential and great chances to achieve a true mature love.

1464. Self-control helps us maintain effective co operations.

1465. Self- control helps us achieve a happy marriage.

1466. In any case it is necessary not to be nervous but controlled.

1467. Self- control is a very valuable quality which must not lack in any person.

1468. Good morale greatly increases our ability to have self-control in any situation.

1469. A man capable of self control in stressing situations has the power and the chances to realize a happy marriage.

1470. Self control must always be promoted, sustained, appreciated, respected and rewarded.

1471. A man with self control knows how to prevent stress.

1472. Those who have high preferences for uncontrollable positive activism have a high potential of achieving a happy life.

1473. Each of us needs to learn how to control our emotions in any situation no matter how surprising or difficult it is.

1474. The self control of emotions is a very valuable quality that helps us a lot in achieving our personal goals.

1475. Those who control circumstances have a high capacity to achieve personal goals.

1476. Those who control circumstances have a great ability to achieve a happy marriage.

1477. People's control of the emotions is a right.

1478. People who can control their emotions are engines of development.

1479. Controlling people's emotions is a necessity.

1480. Those who control circumstances have greater capacities to participate in achieving the greater good.

1481. Those who control circumstances can control them better if they make necessary exchanges of information.

1482. People who can control their emotions have a greater ability to become more efficient.

1483. People who have success have controlled circumstances many times.

1484. People who have success mostly control the necessary discipline to achieve the successes they desire.

1485. Those who control circumstances have a greater potential to succeed.

1486. Those who control circumstances must be promoted.

1487. Those who control circumstances have greater chances of becoming more efficient.

1488. People who can control their emotions have a greater ability to maintain efficient co operations.

1489. People who can control their emotions have a greater capacity of maintaining efficient co-developments.

1490. People who have successes many times maintain their self control.

1491. Those who can control their unconsidered words manage to prevent many arguments.

1492. Those who can control their unconsidered words manage to maintain their marriages happy.

1493.   A man capable of self control in stressing situations has the power and more chances to achieve more and greater successes.

1494.   Those who can't control their unconsidered words manage to maintain true friendships.

1495.   A man capable of self control in stressing situations has the power and more chances to meet more favorable situations.

1496.   A man with self control harmoniously develops his personality.

1497.   We can overcome difficulties that we must overcome also through the formation, development, maintenance and usage of the sense of self control.

1498.   Obtaining as many and great successes that we can, can be achieved through the contribution of formation, development, maintenance and usage of a great ability to self-control ourselves.

1499.   A positive experience can be achieved also through the contribution of the formation, development and maintenance of the ability to self-control.

1500.   In order to stand up once again, be it for the first time, for the second time, for the who knows what time, it is necessary to form, develop, maintain and use the sense of self control.

1501. Our happiness depends largely on the formation, development, maintenance and usage of the ability to control our emotions.

1502. Obtaining as many and great successes that we can, can be achieved through the contribution of formation, development, maintenance and usage of a great capacity to control our emotions no matter how difficult the situation might be.

1503. Desperation can be eliminated also through the contribution of the formation, development, maintenance and usage of the ability to control emotions.

1504. In order to pursue and transform our personal goals into reality we need to form, develop, maintain and use the sense of self control.

1505. We can achieve happiness also through the contribution of the formation, development, maintenance and usage of the ability to have self-control.

1506. In order to change our desire of changing it is a really necessary that we form, develop, maintain and use the sense of self control.

1507. In order to prevent not achieving our personal goals it is necessary to form, develop, maintain and use the ability to control surroundings.

1508. We can overcome the difficulties that we must surpass also through the formation, development, maintenance and usage of the sense of self control.

1509. The desire to make others happy can be achieved through the contribution of the formation, development, maintenance and usage of the sense of self control.

1510. In order to pursue and transform our personal goals into reality we need to form, develop, maintain and use the ability to control oneself.

1511. Will can be formed, developed, maintained and used also through the contribution of the formation, development, maintenance and usage of the capacity of self-control.

1512. Forming wrong ideas can be prevented also through the formation, development, maintenance and usage of self-control.

1513. In order to change it is necessary to form, develop, maintain and use self-control.

1514. Troubles can be prevented through self-control.

1515.   Our happiness depends on the power to control our feelings.

1516.   We can overcome the difficulties that we must overcome also through the formation, development, maintenance and usage of the sense of self control.

1517.   Obtaining as many and greatest successes as we can, can be achieved through the formation, development, maintenance and usage of the great ability to have self-control.

1518.   Positive experience can be achieved also through the contribution of the formation, development and maintenance of the ability of self-control.

1519.   In order to rise up once again for the first time, for the second time, for the who knows what time, it is necessary to form, develop, maintain and use the sense of self control.

1520.   Our happiness depends a lot on the formation, development, maintenance and usage of the ability to control our emotions.

1521.   Positive experience can be achieved also through the contribution of the formation, development and maintenance of the ability to control emotions.

1522. In order to transform positive objectives into reality it is necessary to form, develop, maintain and use the sense of self control.

1523. In order to transform positive objectives into reality it is necessary to form, develop, maintain and use the ability to control our emotions.

1524. In order to pursue and transform positive objectives into reality it is necessary to form, develop, maintain and use the ability to control our emotions.

1525. In order to prevent failures it is necessary that we form, develop, maintain and use the ability to form, develop and maintain positive control.

1526. We can prevent failures also through the contribution of the formation, development, maintenance and usage of self-control behaviors.

1527. Those who can control their unconsidered words manage to prevent many difficulties.

1528. A man with self-control has greater chances to accomplish his personal objectives.

1529. Continuous self-control helps us become respectful.

1530. Some mistakes can be prevented also through the contribution of the formation, development, maintenance and usage of continuous self-controlling behavior.

1531. Continuous self-control helps us become active.

1532. Continuous self-control helps us become tolerant.

1533. Continuous self-control helps us become decisive.

1534. Our happiness depends a lot also on the formation, development, maintenance and usage of continuous self-controlling behavior.

1535. Continuous self-control helps us become spiritual.

1536. Continuous self-control helps us become positive.

1537. Release from our self-imposed restrictions can be made also through the contribution of the formation, development, maintenance and usage of continuous self-control behavior.

1538. Continuous self-motivation helps us become self-controlled.

1539.   Stress can be prevented also through the formation, development, maintenance and usage of self-controlled behavior.

1540.   Hopes can be created also through the contribution of the formation, development, maintenance and usage of continuous self-controlling behavior.

1541.   The force of our ideas can be augmented also through the contribution of the formation, development, maintenance and usage of continuous self-controlling behavior.

1542.   Creativity helps us become self controlled.

1543.   Our happiness depends a lot also on the formation, development, maintenance and usage of self-controlled behavior.

1544.   Continuous self-control helps us become cautious.

1545.   In order to prevent failures it is necessary to also form, develop, maintain and use self-controlled behavior.

1546.   Continuous self-control helps us become adaptable.

1547.   In order to prevent not achieving our personal goals, it is necessary to also form, develop, maintain and use our continuous self-controlling behavior.

1548.   Continuous self-control helps us become unpretentious.

1549.   Hope helps us become self controlling.

1550.   Self-imposed discipline helps us become self controlled.

1551.   The radical transformation for the better of our life can be achieved also through the formation, development, maintenance and usage of self-controlled behavior.

1552.   Continuous self-control helps us become independent.

1553.   In achieving our successes a contribution is also brought by the formation, development, maintenance and usage of continuous control of the self behavior.

1554.   Release from our self-imposed restrictions can be made also through the contribution of the formation, development, maintenance and usage of continuous self-controlling behavior.

1555.   Continuous self-control helps us become peaceful.

1556.   The solutions to the problems we have or that we want to solve can be found also through the contribution of the formation, development, maintenance and usage of self-controlled behavior.

1557.   Continuous self-control helps us become cultivated.

1558.   Rather than lamenting that we do not have successes it is more useful to also form, develop, maintain and use a continuously self-controlled behavior.

1559.   Continuous self-control helps us become docile.

1560.   The force of our ideas can be augmented also through the contribution of the formation, development, maintenance and usage of self-controlled behavior.

1561.   Continuous self-control helps us become charming.

1562.   We can become stronger and we can not allow ourselves to be influenced by the world also through the contribution of the formation, development, maintenance and usage of self-controlled behavior.

1563.   We can overcome the difficulties that we must overcome also through the help of the formation, development, maintenance and usage of self-controlled behavior.

1564.   Continuous self-control helps us become reserved.

1565.   The self efficient use of our time helps us become self controlled.

1566.   Responsibility helps us become self controlled.

1567.   Continuous self-control helps us become pleasant.

1568.   Cherishing oneself helps us become self-controlled.

1569.   Our future can be projected and achieved also through the contribution of the formation, development, maintenance and usage of continuous self-controlling behavior.

1570.   Continuous self-control helps us become content.

1571.   The obstacles that prevent us from achieving our personal goals can be surpassed also through the contribution of the formation, development, maintenance and usage of continuous self-control behavior.

1572.   We can overcome the difficulties that we must overcome also through the help of the formation, development, maintenance and usage of continuous self-controlling behavior.

1573. Continuous self-control helps us become leaders.

1574. We can form, develop and maintain the state of being ourselves also through the contribution of the formation, development, maintenance and usage of a behavior of continuous self-control.

1575. Stress can be prevented also through the formation, development, maintenance and usage of continuous control of the self behavior.

1576. Continuous self-control helps us become funny.

1577. Continuous self-control helps us become enthusiastic.

1578. Rather than lamenting that we do not have successes it is more useful to also form, develop, maintain and use self-controlled behavior.

1579. Communication helps us become self controlled.

1580. Continuous self-control helps us become joyful.

1581.	In order to prevent not achieving our personal goals, it is necessary to also form, develop, maintain and use our continuous control of the self behavior.

1582.	Continuous self-control helps us become friendly.

1583.	Will helps us become self controlled.

1584.	Continuous self-control helps us become decent.

1585.	Some mistakes can be prevented also through the contribution of the formation, development, maintenance and usage of continuous self-control behavior.

1586.	In order to prevent not achieving our personal goals, it is necessary to also form, develop, maintain and use our self-controlled behavior.

1587.	Continuous self-control helps us become ordered.

1588.	Continuous self-control helps us become audacious.

1589.	Wisdom helps us become self controlled.

1590.	Our resistance to changing for the better can be overcome also through the contribution of the formation, development, maintenance and usage of self-controlled behavior.

1591.   The radical transformation for the better of our life can be achieved also through the formation, development, maintenance and usage of continuous control of the self behavior.

1592.   In order to stand up once again for the first time or for the who knows what time, it is necessary to also form, develop, maintain and use a self-controlled behavior.

1593.   Continuous self-control helps us become analytic.

1594.   We can prevent the falling apart of a happy marriage also through the contribution of the formation, development, maintenance and usage of continuous self-controlling behavior.

1595.   Continuous self-control helps us become optimistic.

1596.   Rather than lamenting that we do not have successes it is more useful to also form, develop, maintain and use a continuously control of the self behavior.

1597.   Continuous self-control helps us become initiating.

1598.   Continuous self-control helps us become harmless.

1599.   Stress can be prevented also through the formation, development, maintenance and usage of continuous self-controlling behavior.

1600.   Continuous self-control helps us become energetic.

1601.   Continuous self-control helps us become flexible.

1602.   We can prevent the falling apart of a happy marriage also through the contribution of the formation, development, maintenance and usage of self-controlled behavior.

1603.   Continuous self-control helps us become daring.

1604.   Aspiring towards a more meaningful life can also be achieved through the formation, development, maintenance and usage of continuous self-controlling behavior.

1605.   Continuous self-control helps us become selfless.

1606.   Continuous self-control helps us become trained.

1607.   Continuous self perfection helps us become self-controlled.

1608.   Continuous self-control helps us become bold.

Correct

1609.   Our happiness is sometimes influenced by our correct or incorrect perception of our situation.

1610.   Envy is an incorrect behavior that damages us, and sometimes it can cause us enormously much damage.

1611.   Enmities are incorrect behaviors that damage, sometimes, both us, as well as those who are our enemies.

1612.   Only by making a correct hierarchy, all the time, of our personal goals, according to importance and urgency, we can achieve more personal goals.

1613.   Correctly and realistically establishing our objectives helps us a lot to achive more bigger or smaller successes.

1614.   Incorrect behavior of the husband towards his wife leads to decreased confidence of the wife in the husband.

1615.   The correct behavior of a husband towards his wife leads to increased confidence in him by his wife.

1616.   Those who are correct have fewer failures.

1617.   Those who are correct are less wrong.

1618.   If as a result of failure or multiple failures we change the target following a correct analysis, it does not mean that we are faint-hearted.

1619.   It is not correct to make fun of those who have ideas that we do not understand.

1620.   The more correct we are to those around us the more chances we have to make more friends.

1621.   Correct relations of friendship make us happy and have positive effects on our health.

1622.   If we have a right to know the correct laws, the correct interpretation of laws and persistence this helps us win law suits.

1623.   The judge should be obliged to apply the law correctly, not the way he wants, as unfortunately there are still many judges in the world who do that.

1624.   We are enormously wrong always when we hurry and get immediate answers to some questions without analysis, thinking and seeking the answers correctly.

1625.   Incorrect behavior of the husband towards the wife leads to decreased confidence in her husband.

1626. Correct behavior of the wife towards the husband leads to increased confidence in her husband.

1627. Anger is an incorrect behavior with multiple negative effects.

1628. The work of correct journalists must be supported by all of us, appreciated and rewarded at its just value, according to the case.

1629. The correct behavior of a man towards his wife and other members of his family makes that man be very respected by his wife and members of his family.

1630. The correct establishing of objectives helps achieve them.

1631. The correct setting of goals helps us achieve efficient co operations.

1632. In life, we must not behave like x or y says, but according to the way we think it is best, positive, correct, legal and human.

1633. When we have correctly established our personal goals we have the possibility to more efficiently manage our time.

1634. Correct thinking helps us a lot in achieving true friendships.

1635. Correct relations with coworkers help us achieve more harmonious social relations.

1636. The sense of responsibility contributes a lot in achieving some correct social relations.

1637. Problems cannot be solved by the ideas that created them but through other ideas and through the contribution of formation, development, maintenance, and the usage of correct thinking.

1638. In order to take correct decisions it is necessary to form, develop, maintain and use the ability to be responsible.

1639. Problems cannot be solved by the ideas of that created them but also through the contribution of the formation, development, maintenance and usage of correct thinking.

1640. In order to trace and transform our personal goals into reality it is necessary that we form and develop correct thinking.

1641. Forming wrong ideas can be prevented also through the formation, development, maintenance and usage of correct thinking.

1642. Preventing the formation of doubts can be achieved also through the formation, development, maintenance and usage of a correct life conception.

1643. We can replace wrong ideas with correct ideas also through the contribution of the formation, development, maintenance and usage of a positive life conception.

1644. Those who have high objectives in life mostly have a correct thinking.

1645. Persons who have not succeeded in building a happy marriage up to a certain date, in order to succeed they need to form and develop a correct thinking.

1646. People who know how to take quality decisions also have a correct thinking.

1647. Most of those who know how to prevent possible mistakes also have a correct thinking.

1648. Those who have the obligation to choose correctly must not be underestimated.

1649. The sense of achievement and quality in everything we do imposes the using of a correct thinking.

1650. People who have had successes mostly have a correct thinking.

1651. Preventing the formation of doubts can be achieved also through the formation, development, maintenance and usage of correct thinking.

1652.	We can replace wrong ideas with correct ideas also through the contribution of the formation, development, maintenance and usage of realistic thinking.

1653.	We can prevent breaking a happy marriage also through the contribution of the formation, development, maintenance and usage of correct behaviors.

1654.	In order to take correct decisions it is necessary to form, develop, maintain and use the ability to efficiently plan positive actions.

1655.	Preventing stress can be achieved also through the contribution of the formation, development, maintenance and usage of correct behaviors.

1656.	Emancipation from self imposed restrictions can be done also through the contribution of the formation, development, maintenance and usage of correct thinking.

1657.	Rather than lamenting that we do not have successes it is better to form, develop and maintain correct thinking.

1658.	The desire to make others happy can be achieved through the contribution of the formation, development, maintenance and usage of correct thinking.

1659.   We can replace wrong ideas with correct ideas also through the contribution of the formation, development, maintenance and usage of constructive ideas.

1660.   Correct thinking can be formed, developed, maintained and used also through the contribution of the formation, development, maintenance and usage of correct ideas.

1661.   Preventing stress can be achieved also through the contribution of the formation, development, maintenance and usage of a correct behavior.

1662.   In order to pursue and transform our personal goals into reality we need to form and develop correct thinking.

1663.   We can replace wrong ideas with the correct ideas also through the contribution of the formation, development, maintenance and usage of a positive life conception.

1664.   The solutions to the problems we have we can find also through the contribution of the formation, development, maintenance and usage of correct thinking.

1665.   In order to take corrective decisions it is necessary to form, develop, maintain and use the ability to react with understanding.

1666.   Our happiness depends a lot on the formation, development, maintenance and usage of the ability to constantly choose correctly.

1667.   Forming the wrong ideas about what is happening to us can be prevented also through the contribution of the formation, development, maintenance and usage of correct thinking.

1668.   Forming wrong ideas can be prevented also through the formation, development, maintenance and usage of the ability to select correct ideas from wrong ideas.

1669.   In order to pursue and transform our personal goals into reality we need to form, develop, maintain and use correct thinking as well.

1670.   In order to change our desire of changing it is a really necessary that we form, develop, maintain and use correct thinking.

1671.   In order to escape poverty it is necessary to form, develop, maintain and use correct thinking.

1672.   Efficient ideas are always correct ideas.

1673.   Forming around ideas can be prevented through the contribution of the formation, development, maintenance and usage of correct ideas.

1674. Our own personality can be maintained through the correct decisions we make.

1675. The meaning of life can be found through the contribution of the formation, development, maintenance and usage of correct ideas.

1676. We can replace wrong ideas with correct ideas through finding and using correct ideas.

1677. A correct thinking can be formed by using logical thinking.

1678. Pessimism can be removed through the contribution of the formation, development, maintenance and usage of correct thinking.

1679. We can prevent the falling apart of a happy marriage also through the contribution of the formation, development, maintenance and usage of correct behaviors.

1680. Emancipation from restrictions can be made through the formation, development, maintenance and usage of correct thinking.

1681. Forming wrong ideas can be prevented through the contribution of the formation, development, maintenance and usage of correct thinking.

1682.	In order not to let ourselves be overwhelmed by the difficulties of life it is necessary to form, develop, maintain and use a correct life conception.

1683.	We can make correct decisions if we know ourselves.

1684.	Emancipation from restrictions can be achieved if we use our time correctly.

1685.	Stress can be prevented also through the contribution of the formation, development, maintenance and usage of correct behaviors.

1686.	We can replace wrong ideas with correct ideas also through the contribution of the formation, development, maintenance and usage of efficient ideas.

1687.	Forming vices can be prevented also through the contribution of the formation, development, maintenance and usage of correct behaviors.

1688.	Correct thinking can be formed, developed and used also through the contribution of the formation, development, maintenance and usage of all only objective ideas.

1689. We can become stronger and we cannot let ourselves be influenced by the world also through the contribution of the formation, development, maintenance and usage of a correct life conception.

1690. Developing our thinking can be achieved also through the formation, development, maintenance and usage of a correct life conception.

1691. The way we see life can be correct or not.

1692. Mutual correct appreciations maintain friendships.

1693. Illegal accusations can be prevented by effective laws and their correct application.

1694. People want to be appreciated correctly.

1695. He who makes correct appreciations is appreciated a lot by people.

1696. He who makes correct appreciations is esteemed by people.

1697. Correct appreciations are appreciated a lot.

1698. Our way of seeing love relations can be correct or incorrect.

1699. AGC mediations help us become more correct.

1700.   Successes in life can also be achieved thanks to the correct establishment of our personal goals.

1701.   Our chances of becoming happy increase if we are correctly organize.

Danger

1702.   Dehumanization is very dangerous to society.

1703.   Organized state crime is the most dangerous crime because it is conducted by officials of state and elected officials, other staff working for the state or on behalf of the state and they are using their function in avhieving the crime of using their function, institution and other institutions of the state.

1704.   Corruption is so generalized in the world and so harmful that it constitutes a global danger of humanity, the greatest and the most dangerous and with negative effects that it creates for society.

1705.   The man whom you can not trust is dangerous.

1706.   Hatred is extremely dangerous.

1707.   Revenge is extremely dangerous.

1708. A man without judgement is extremely dangerous.

1709. Stupidity is extremely dangerous.

1710. Pettiness is extremely dangerous.

1711. Waste is extremely dangerous.

1712. Envy is a cancer, very dangerous, it eats us on the inside.

1713. Discrimination is a very dangerous factor of stress.

1714. He who is irrational is extremely dangerous.

1715. The foolish man is extremely dangerous.

1716. Artfulness is a very dangerous flaw.

1717. The man who is sick is extremely dangerous.

1718. Hypocrisy is extremely dangerous.

1719. The man who does not even know what is good for him is extremely dangerous.

1720. Boorishness is an extremely dangerous flaw.

1721. The man who is irrational is extremely dangerous.

1722. A man who is careless about himself and about others is dangerous.

1723. A man who is careless and without objectives is a danger to himself.

1724. Laziness a dangerous defect.

1725. A lying man is extremely dangerous.

1726. The man that you can not trust is dangerous.

1727. Corrupt politicians are very dangerous; they are like viruses.

1728. Human stupidity is incredibly dangerous most of the times.

1729. The quality of sensing situations helps us a lot to discover danger.

1730. Political corruption is a very great danger to democracy.

1731. The quality of sensing situations helps us a lot to avoid dangers.

1732. Those who have high objectives in life know how to overcome the dangers that come in life most of the times.

1733. People who have had successes have known how to cope with many dangers.

Decision

1734. When we are doubtful we must find solutions to get rid of indecision.

1735. Indecision can sometimes harm us very much.

1736. Decision prevents failure many times.

1737. Decision leads us to success.

1738. Young people have the right and obligation to participate directly or indirectly through their representatives in decisions making that affect them directly and indirectly,

1739. It is necessary and required thet states create legislative conditions for the application of organisational, financial laws, so that young people and can use resources in central and local decision-making, participate in making central and local decision-making, and participate in their implementation.

1740. Mental self-development increases our efficiency with which we take personal decisions for others and for society, it greatly enhances the quality of the decisions we make, it greatly enhances the quality of our personal actions and those that co-ordinate them.

1741.   he capacity to take rapid decisions increases our possibilities to achieve a more beautiful life.

1742.   The ability to make rapid decisions increases our possibilities to achieve efficient co operations.

1743.   An illegal decision must not be applied.

1744.   Most of the decisions that are not documented properly are wrong decisions.

1745.   People who take positive decisions have greater chances to achieve their own happiness.

1746.   Persons who take positive decisions have greater chances to achieve efficient co operations.

1747.   People who take positive decisions contribute a lot to achieving the greater good.

1748.   Persons who take positive decisions use more information.

1749.   People who take positive decisions must be supported.

1750.   Persons who take positive decisions contribute a lot in achieving a positive global future.

1751. People who take positive decisions contribute a lot in maintaining true friendships.

1752. People who take positive decisions have more and greater chances to achieve their personal goals.

1753. Persons who take positive decisions have more chances to maintain a mature love.

1754. People who take positive decisions must be rewarded.

1755. Skilled people mostly take positive decisions.

1756. The simplicity of decisions allows them to be taken in a short period of time.

1757. The simplicity of decisions allows you to take quality decisions.

1758. The simplicity of decisions makes them more easily applicable.

1759. The simplicity of decisions makes them more easily understood.

1760. Most of the decisions taken without the necessary research are wrong.

1761. An illegal decision cannot be applied.

1762. People who take positive decisions are also engines of progress in all areas of activity.

1763. People who take positive decisions have more chances to succeed in life.

1764. People who take positive decisions can participate more rapidly in efficient global co operations.

1765. People who take positive decisions must be appreciated.

1766. The persons that take positive decisions must be promoted.

1767. The state of uncertainty stops the making of decisions very much.

1768. The state of uncertainty causes postponing the taking of some decisions.

1769. People who have success have a great capacity of rapidly taking decisions.

1770. The majority of the decisions taken at first sight are wrong.

1771. Wrong decisions must be revealed as being wrong as soon as possible.

1772. A wrong decision must not be applied.

1773. A decision, in order to be fair must be legal also.

1774.   An illegal decision must be changed with a good decision as soon as possible.

1775.   Many well-known failures are due to wrong decisions.

1776.   The majority of decisions have both positive effects as well as negative effects.

1777.   Decisions must be taken so as to have a maximum of few negative effects.

1778.   Before taking a decision we must build and consider all possible effects that it can have, both negative and positive ones.

1779.   Those who know how to take positive decisions have more and greater successes.

1780.   People who know how to take positive decisions can perfect themselves.

1781.   People who take positive decisions are engines of development.

1782.   We each have the right to take a positive decision.

1783.   We each have the obligation to take a positive decision.

1784.   It is a necessity that each of us takes a positive decision.

1785. People who take positive decisions have more and greater chances to achieve their desired future.

1786. People who take positive decisions are mostly credible.

1787. People who take positive decisions mostly have few mistakes and even zero mistakes.

1788. People who take positive decisions have greater and more chances to achieve themselves.

1789. The majority of people who take positive decisions more easily maintain the positive social relations that they have.

1790. Those who have objectives in life mostly take efficient decisions.

1791. All of those who know how to prevent possible mistakes have a greater ability of taking quality decisions.

1792. Hesitating behavior reduces the operability of the decisions that we take.

1793. Our ability of taking rapid decisions helps us have more chances to meet favorable situations.

1794. The ability of taking the rapid decisions increases our efficiency a lot.

1795.   Most people who have had successes know how to take rapid decisions.

1796.   The ability to take rapid decisions increases our possibilities of achieving our personal goals a lot faster.

1797.   The ability to take rapid decisions increases our capacity of achieving outstanding performances.

1798.   Young people need and must implicate themselves in taking all the decisions that affect them directly or indirectly.

1799.   The ability to take rapid decisions increases our chances to achieve efficient co-developments.

1800.   The ability to take rapid decisions helps us achieve true friendships.

1801.   A lie, defined truth through definite court decision, cannot become the truth, because the definite court decision is a false and a felony resulted from many felonies committed by the judge who, in bad faith, has illegally turned a lie into the truth through an illegal and false definite court order.

1802.   Wrong ideas produce wrong decisions.

1803.   The ability to take rapid decisions increases our possibilities to prevent many unpleasant surprises.

1804.   In order to take correct decisions it is necessary to form, develop, maintain and use the ability to be responsible.

1805.   Obtaining more and greater successes can be achieved also through the contribution of the formation, development, maintenance and usage of a greater capacity to take rapid quality decisions.

1806.   In order to trace and transform our personal objectives into reality it is necessary to form, develop, maintain and use the ability to take rapid quality decisions.

1807.   The simplicity of decisions makes these decisions be more quickly understood.

1808.   Those who have high goals in life mostly take efficient decisions.

1809.   People who know how to take quality decisions react with trust.

1810.   Those who have high objectives in life mostly have the ability to take rapid decisions.

1811.   In order to pursue and transform our personal goals into reality we need to form and develop the ability of knowing how to take quality decisions.

1812.   Positive experience can be achieved also to the contribution of the formation, and development and maintenance of the ability to take rapid quality decisions.

1813.   In order to change the desire of changing into reality it is necessary to form, develop, maintain and use the ability to take rapid quality decisions.

1814.   In order to take correct decisions it is necessary to form, develop, maintain and use the ability to efficiently plan positive actions.

1815.   Troubles can be prevented also through the contribution of the formation, development, maintenance and usage of the ability to take rapid decisions.

1816.   Obtaining as many and great successes that we can can be achieved through the contribution of formation, development, maintenance and usage of a great ability to rapidly take quality decisions.

1817.   In order to pursue and transform our personal goals into reality we need to form, develop, maintain and use the ability to take rapid quality decisions.

1818.   In order to take corrective decisions it is necessary to form, develop, maintain and use the ability to react with understanding.

1819.   In order to take correct decisions we need to form, develop, maintain and use the ability to solve problems legally.

1820.   Emancipation from self imposed restrictions can be made through the formation, development and maintenance of the ability to take rapid quality decisions.

1821.   Forming wrong ideas can be prevented also through the formation, development, maintenance and usage of the ability to take rapid quality decisions.

1822.   In order to take correct decisions it is necessary that we form, develop, maintain and use the ability to be responsible.

1823.   In order to pursue and transform our personal goals into reality we need to form and develop the ability to take rapid quality decisions.

1824.   In order to take fair decisions we must dissociate emotions.

1825.   The state of psychical discomfort can be removed through the formation, development and maintenance of the ability to take rapid quality decisions.

1826.   Our own personality can be maintained through the correct decisions we make.

1827.   Our transformation for the better can be achieved through the ability to rapidly take quality decisions.

1828.   In order to pursue and transform positive objectives into reality it is necessary to form and develop the ability to know how to take quality decisions.

1829.   A positive experience can be achieved also through the contribution of the formation, development and maintenance of the ability to rapidly take quality decisions.

1830.   We can make correct decisions if we know ourselves.

1831.   The ability to take rapid and good decisions ensures success.

1832.   The accumulation of all data necessary for taking right decisions helps us achieve more performances.

1833.   The great capacity of taking efficient decisions helps us achieve more pleasant surprises.

1834.   The great capacity of taking efficient decisions helps us achieve more efficient co operations.

Delicate

1835.   The woman is a delicate being, that all men
        want to have, they need to understand her in
        order to achieve a true love, a mature and
        happy marriage with happy children.

Desire

1836.   Through a positive thinking we can
        overcome our desires.

1837.   Our desires are very numerous in some and
        no less numerous in others. In fact, if we
        had wishes limted only to the realistic and
        possible ones to achieve, we will fulfill them
        if we will act to satisfy them or not.

1838.   The more subjective desires are, unlimited
        by logical criteria, realistic, the more they
        can not be solved or can sometimes be
        solved with some very large negative effects
        on our lives. Some people achieve them
        even if the achievement of these subjective
        desires harm them more or less in one or
        several ways.

1839.   The more subjective desires are, unlimited
        by logical criteria, realistic, the more they
        can not be solved or can sometimes be
        solved with some very large negative effects
        on our lives. Some people achieve them
        even if the achievement of these subjective

desires harm them more or less in one or several ways.

1840.   In order to achieve some personal desires some people do not even have the minimum necessary common sense.

1841.   The inner beauty of a woman along with the inner beauty of a man contributes the most in achieving the joint happiness that each desires.

1842.   We must have the power to be strong enough and select achievable desires from those are unreachable and transform them into personal objectives.

Difficult

1843.   True friendship can help us pass much easier over the many difficulties of life, and it would not be so if it did not exist.

1844.   In any situation, no matter how difficult it would be, it is necessary to have a responsible behavior.

1845.   In any difficult situation, no matter how difficult it is, it is necessary not to lose our self control, our temper.

1846.   He who is unpleasent makes friends more difficultly.

1847.   Perseverance is a special quality that helps us achieve many bigger or smaller successes, face any difficulties, cavils, obstacles, achieve outstanding performances, achieve our objectives, become happy, achieve and maintain a happy marriage .

1848.   True friends are those who wish you well, cooperate with you when you need to, who are there by your side in every good and bad situation. They are those people who do not leave in exceptional circumstances, the most difficult ones of your life.

1849.   True friends give us security, increase our safety, make us feel better, create a lot of satisfactions, joy, much happiness, help us cooperate to get through many difficulties of life, to achieve outstanding performances, to achieve the objectives etc. These contributions of theirs are invaluable to us. In turn it is necessary, useful and well of us to also be true friends to them both for their sake and for our sake and happiness.

1850.   We can face and overcome difficulties much easier in life with the more we accumulate from books, the Internet; more useful and necessary knowledge for surpassing the troubles we face in life.

1851.   True friendship helps us, in need, in dealing with the difficulties that appear in front of us.

1852.   The more true the friends we have are, the more power we accumulate. This power helps us cope with the difficulties we have to overcome even the unfair hits we receive.

Discipline

1853.   Those who are disciplined are less wrong.

1854.   The rigorous and disciplined at work have much greater opportunities to obtain and maintain employment. Rigor and discipline at the workplace can be easy if we want to, if we do not have it. Rigor and discipline are two keys to getting a job if you do not have it, or if we have one, they are keys to keeping it. Good luck.

1855.   The disciplined man is an engine of progress in all the fields of activity.

1856.   Self imposed discipline helps us and contributes a lot to forming social relations.

1857.   He who is disciplined is appreciated, respected and rewarded.

1858.   We can make our life more beautiful if we are disciplined.

1859.   If we are indisciplined we will have many failures in life.

1860. In everything we do we need to be disciplined. We all know this but unfortunately many of us do not respect it in many situations.

1861. Discipline in everything we do helps us very much to achieve personal goals faster.

1862. Discipline in what we do help us very much to have more chances to meet more favorable situations.

1863. Those who know that discipline is one of the keys of dreams have a greater capacity of achieving more and greater outstanding performances.

1864. People who know how to take quality decisions have and develop their sense of self-imposed discipline.

1865. Discipline creates discipline.

1866. A disciplined man has a greater potential to achieve a happy life.

1867. Self imposed discipline contributes a lot in achieving some very efficient global co operations.

1868. Self imposed discipline helps us and contributes a lot to achieve a happy life.

1869. People with the sense of discipline have a great capacity to succeed in life.

1870. People with the sense of discipline have greater chances to achieve their own happiness.

1871. People with the sense of discipline more easily achieve social relations.

1872. Those who know discipline is the key of dreams have more chances to achieve their desired future.

1873. Those who know that discipline is the key of dreams have a greater ability to succeed in life.

1874. Those who know that discipline is one of the keys of dreams have the ability to maintain their desired efficient co-developments.

1875. Those who know that discipline is one of the keys of dreams have a greater ability to achieve a happy marriage.

1876. Those who have high objectives in life have the ability and the sense of self imposed quality discipline.

1877. Self imposed discipline contributes a lot to achieving the future.

1878. Self imposed discipline helps us and contributes a lot to finding our suited partner for life.

1879.   A disciplined man has a greater potential to achieve more and greater outstanding performances.

1880.   Self-imposed discipline helps us a lot to prevent mistakes.

1881.   Self-imposed discipline helps us a lot to achieve a true mature love.

1882.   Self-imposed discipline can be obtained through experiences, through practice, through imitating, through learning, etc.

1883.   Discipline must be appreciated, promoted and supported.

1884.   Self-imposed discipline helps us and contributes a lot to achieving outstanding performances.

1885.   Discipline can be formed, developed, maintained and used through the contribution of the formation, development, maintenance and usage of the ability of organization.

1886.   In order to trace and transform our personal objectives into reality it is necessary to form, develop, maintain and use the sense of discipline in everything we do.

1887.   People with the sense of discipline have a great capacity to achieve efficient co operations.

1888.   Those who know discipline is the key of dreams have a great capacity to achieve more and greater outstanding performances.

1889.   Those who know that discipline is the key of dreams have the ability to maintain the social relations they desire.

1890.   Those who know that discipline is one of the keys of dreams have the ability to achieve mature love.

1891.   The desire to make others happy can really be achieved also through the contribution of the formation, development, maintenance and usage of the sense of self imposed discipline.

1892.   Forming wrong ideas can be prevented also through the formation, development, maintenance and usage of self-imposed discipline.

1893.   In order to change the desire of changing into reality it is necessary to form, develop, maintain and use the ability to impose yourselves with the necessary discipline.

1894.   Problems cannot only be solved by the ideas of that created them but also through the contribution of the formation, development, maintenance and usage of behavior is of self-imposed discipline.

1895. Problems cannot only be solved by the ideas of that created them but also through the contribution of the formation, development, maintenance and usage of behaviors of self-imposed discipline.

1896. In achieving successes a contribution is brought by the formation, development, maintenance and usage of behaviors that respect self-imposed discipline.

1897. In order to pursue and transform our personal goals into reality we need to form, develop, maintain and use the sense of discipline in everything we do.

1898. Discipline can be formed, developed, maintained and used also through the contribution of the formation, development, maintenance and usage of the sense of responsibility.

1899. We can overcome the difficulties that we must surpass also through the formation, development, maintenance and usage of the sense of self-imposed discipline.

1900. Discipline can be formed, developed, maintained and used also through the contribution of the formation, development, maintenance and usage of self-imposed discipline.

1901. In order to pursue and transform our personal goals into reality we need to form, develop, maintain and use self-imposed discipline.

1902. Discipline can be formed, developed, maintained and used also through the contribution of the formation, development, maintenance and usage of the ability to organize.

1903. Discipline can be formed also through the involvement in efficient projects.

1904. Our transformation for the better can be achieved through discipline.

1905. Finding the meaning of life can be achieved through discipline.

1906. Problems cannot be solved by the ideas that created them but also through the contribution of the formation, development, maintenance and usage of Self-imposed disciplined behaviors.

1907. In order to change into reality it is necessary to form, develop, maintain and use the sense of discipline.

1908.   Discipline can be formed, developed and maintained by efficiently planning actions.

1909.   Successes are achieved if we are disciplined.

1910.   Ignorance can be fought by using discipline.

1911.   Discipline creates many successes.

1912.   Without discipline we cannot achieve outstanding successes.

1913.   Self-impose discipline must not disturb us in any way.

1914.   Discipline prevents many unpleasant surprises.

1915.   Self-imposed discipline helps us a lot to become more efficient.

1916.   Discipline prevents much trouble.

1917.   Self-imposed discipline helps us a lot to achieve our personal goals.

1918.   Those who know that discipline is the key of dreams have the potential to achieve their own happiness.

1919.   Those who know that discipline is one of the keys of dreams have a greater ability to find the right partner for life.

Distant

1920. We all think about what we will do in the next or more distant days.

1921. Our distanced future can be greatly influenced by what we do in the future before that distant future.

1922. The more distant the future is the more the factors that will influence it will be more numerous and some more unknown to us.

1923. Our distant future can be changed more or less by what we decide now, primarily for our continuing concern of building a certain future of the great changes taking place in society, of the relations, the contacts that we have with various people, of the information that we come in contact with, of the depth and accuracy of the analysis of information we come in contact with, of the creative capacity of our ideas to create new projects, new objectives in the light of our experience, our present , the information we fiind and receive etc.

1924. Our orientation towards a very distant future is a creative attitude that helps us a lot to achieve our personal goals.

1925. A man with an orientation towards the distant future has greater and more chances to achieve outstanding performances.

1926. He who is very distant makes true friends very hard.

1927. A man oriented towards the distant future has more and greater chances to become more efficient.

Effect

1928. Necessary and useful ideas to us - it is effective and necessary to us to admire, ordere, etc..them in books so that we can find them more easily and quickly in need.

1929. To become champions in a field it is necessary to act effectively by abiding by the rules which, if respected, make us champions.

1930. Discrimination can be prevented quickly and effectively in the world through solidarity and unity.

1931. Most of the time long term thinking is more effective than short-term thinking.

1932. Long term thinking is often more effective than short-term thinking.

1933. Periodic analysis of our actions is very necessary to help us increase the effectiveness of future actions.

1934. Literacy is extremely effective to society.

1935.   Illiteracy has many negative effects both for the illiterate and for society.

1936.   Positive facts have multiple positive effects.

1937.   If we have children, in order to prevent divorce and its negative effects, it is necessary for scientists to pay more attention to studying family relationships and family.

1938.   From now on, mankind has sufficient resources to address poverty in an incredibly short time by mobilizing and effectively using all existing resources.

1939.   Our time must be used most effectively and not wasted.

1940.   Although our time is very precious to us, most of us do not use it effectively.

1941.   The effective management of our time is a special quality.

1942.   The effective management of our time is a necessary quality.

1943.   In achieving our objectives it is necessary to find and use effectively all the possibilities.

1944.   Preventive actions are very effective in most cases.

1945.   The effective idea is a part of the effective
         action.

1946.   Each of us has far greater opportunities to
         become more effective than we think.

1947.   The aid given at the necessary time often
         has incredible positive effects.

1948.   Things go better when we act effectively.

1949.   An effective self control of our thinking leads
         us to happiness.

1950.   By acting continuously and effectively to
         achieve positive goals we will surely achieve
         them.

1951.   Some successes are the effects of beliefs.

1952.   Successes are also effects of our
         experience.

1953.   Successes are also effects of positive
         thinking.

1954.   Unity is a factor of many effective co
         operations.

1955.   Understanding is a factor of many effective
         co operations.

1956.   The effects of human actions have an
         increasing influence on the environment.
         This makes us think on a global scale, long-

term and scientific before acting and makes us perform more profound studies, of impact, regarding our actions, to prevent the implementation of actions that have negative, inadmissible effects on the environment, society and people.

1957.   We can prevent more failures if we analyze our actions, their positive and negative effects, so that we and others achieve and avoid actions with negative, risky, illegal effects.

1958.   Today, most people do not use their ability to think but very little and ineffectively.

1959.   Humor has positive effects on health.

1960.   By acting continuously and effectively to making a happy marriage, we shall achieve it.

1961.   Happiness has positive effects on health.

1962.   Only effective actions can help us obtain many bigger or smaller successes.

1963.   Most young people do not use the energy of youth effectively, for themselves, but they waste it in vain.

1964.   Sometimes, our hastiness makes us make very big mistakes, with large negative effects, both for us and for others. So, beware, let us always avoid hastily behavior.

1965. When we are tired, it is better and effective to relax for several reasons. One is that when we are tired we make more mistakes than when we are rested.

1966. Rather than to work when we are tired, it is better to rest, because much wrong and some mistakes can be fatal or can have enormous negative effects depending on the work that we do at that time.

1967. As we become more effective the more opportunities we have of achieving more successes.

1968. The development and practical application of the science of preventing human errors would have positive effects for all people in the world, incalculable, many, very deep, very different, incredible effects.

1969. It is necessary to create and develop very rapidly the science of effective usage by man of all resources available to man.

1970. The negative effects for that or those wrongly accused should be borne by the one or ones who have wrongly accused him and the proper moral damages should also.

1971.   The effective man has possibilities due to his effectiveness of becoming more effective.

1972.   The effective man will carry out effectively in his life much more success than the ineffective man.

1973.   The effective man is effective in creating happiness.

1974.   The effective man has great chances of achieving high performances.

1975.   The more effective we become, the more we have a greater chance to obtain greater and more successes.

1976.   Before publishing, those who write need to analyze the positive and negative effects of what they publicize.

1977.   Human knowledge should be used effectively, organized, planned, impersonal, humanist for the good of our people and, in an incredibly short time, the quality of life of billions of people would grow incredibly much.

1978.   Those who are most effectively active have much greater opportunities to achieve success.

1979. Acting continuously and effectively to achieve positive goals we will surely achieve them.

1980. It is always necessary to be effective in any situation because in this way we are able to achieve more bigger or smaller successes and a lot of enjoyment, joy, happiness.

1981. Objectivity is essential to effective and positive actions.

1982. Inattention can often have very big negative effects.

1983. Corruption is so generalized in the world and so harmful that it constitutes a global danger of humanity, the greatest and the most dangerous and with negative effects that it creates for society.

1984. The loss of family ties, enormous harms the one who lost them, sometimes having some very large negative effects for that person, unbalancing his life.

1985. Loneliness is very harmful to those who are lonely, it has more negative effects on the lonely person.

1986. Alcoholism is a primary cause of many divorces; it has negative effects on the family.

1987. Where it comes to divorce, where there are children, it is necessary that the relations between former spouses be so that the effects of divorce affect children as less as possible.

1988. Positive and effective ideas definitely lead us in achieving our objectives.

1989. The art of living can be learned through will, persistence, continuing education and effective actions to achieve the objectives.

1990. A positive, effective way of life makes our life happy.

1991. Every day we have the same 24 hours, but vary greatly according to the efficiency or inefficiency daily use of those 24 hours. Those who use it most effectively progress the most.

1992. Using more effectively 24 hours daily needs to be a permanent objective of ours.

1993. We need, in order to accumulate knowledge very valuable to us and to achieving our objectives to listen to people who have achieved success, those who have knowledge that we need. No matter how we come in contact with them: directly, by radio, television, the Internet, it is very effective for us to take such useful, sometimes very useful information, knowledge to us for free.

1994. The more effective use of our time should be a priority objective for us, urgent and important for as long as we live, because it is very important in achieving all the objectives of our present and future.

1995. In order to be able to more effectively use our time it is necessary to have continuously set present and future goals for the future.

1996. We can learn from the others' positive effective behaviors free of charge, by observing their positive, effective, human behavior. Many of the behaviors that we learn by observation can help us greatly to increase the efficiency of the use of our time, to increase the efficiency of our actions, to achieve faster objectives of our present and future.

1997. Permanently, every day, it is very useful to expand the effectiveness of our self-lesrning.

1998. In life we may each receive more or less unjust blows. No unjust blow should consume us, because if we consume ourselves we do not solve anything but instead we harm us and sometimes even very much and we also complicate some problems that we have.

1999. First of all when we receive an unjust blow, we should focus on finding solutions, actions

236

to help us minimize the negative effects of the blow, unless we can reduce them to zero.

2000. Secondly, it is necessary to identify the causes and factors that led us to receiving them unjustly.

2001. Thirdly, it is necessary to remove the causes that led us to receiving them unjustly, so that we shall not receive them again or several times again.

2002. In the fourth line is necessary to take all necessary measures to prevent the causes that led us to reciving the X blow unjustly.

2003. Fifthly it is necessary to seek to identify whether there are other causes that might lead us to receive further blows unjustly.

2004. Sixthly it is necessary to discover other potential causes that could cause us to receive more unfair blows by taking the necessary measures: 1) to eliminate these causes, 2) where we can not prevent these causes it is necessary to take the necessary measures not to receive them unjustly, 3) if we receive them, to make the blow have as little negative effects as possible over us.

2005. In the seventh line it is necessary that our new situation caused by the unfair blow is used efficiently for us. It is possible that what we accomplish after the new situation created by the unjustly received blow is much larger and beneficial to us than the achievements that we had done if we had not received the blow unjustly.

2006. For those who have many great successes we can always learn more effective behaviors that may lead us and to many and great successes.

2007. By studying how they manage time, those people who have had many and great successes can help us learn more effective behaviors than ours.

2008. From now on, mankind has enough resources to solve the problem of illiteracy in a record time, an incredibly short one by mobilizing and effectively use all of our existing resources.

2009. We continuously expand the effectiveness of positive thinking.

2010. A goal of our life should be the continuous increasing of the effectiveness of positive thinking.

2011. Investments made by each country effectively in the creation and development of creative thinking and ability will be the most effective investment that can be made, for several reasons. In addition the positive effects of investing in the creation and development of creative thinking and ability will enable it to allocate sufficient funds to achieve the objectives of creating and developing creative thinking and ability.

2012. Effective preventive actions are very efficient in most cases.

2013. Effective preventive thinking can create many ideas that become effective preventive measures and can contribute greatly to the achievement of personal goals.

2014. The effective idea is a part of the effective action that generated it.

2015. Only effective useful ideas lead us to achieving some bigger or smaller successes.

2016. To achieve personal goals it is necessary to effectively find and use all the resources that help us achieve them.

2017. We can prevent errors through a better organization, and more effective personal actions.

2018. Some of the unthought-of actions of people have very high and multiple negative effects.

2019. If some people are reckless and have as a will the determining the personal goals of becoming prudent and if they continuously act effectively to achieve this personal objective, they will become prudent.

2020.   Happiness can be achieved much easier and much faster if we set as a personal goal to live to be happy and to act effectively on a continuous basis to achieve it. Without having this objective the chances of being happy are much smaller.

2021.   Each of us we could have more joy, more satisfaction and happiness, if we used more effectively our resources.

2022.   Many of us still use our time more inefficiently than we can. Each of us has very large reserves and resources to greatly expand the effectiveness of using our time and we should use them to continually expand the efficiency of our time.

2023.   In our time, most poor people can escape poverty by using the abilities they possess more efficiently, by preventing inefficient actions and flaws and by looking for effective solutions and actions.

2024.   Understanding maintains effective co operations.

2025.   Mental self-development enormously increases with much efficiency, productivity our actions with tremendous positive effects so that we can cooperate with others and with society.

2026. In life we evolve very much as if we set for as long as we live a personal goal and objective to develop and move continuously, organized, planned and effective ways to achieve it.

2027. In everyday life we find a lot of live models, who have as a personal goal to evolve, which have achieved many bigger or smaller successes, joy and much happiness and satisfaction from whom we can take many effective positive behaviors to help us greatly in achieving our objective to evolve and to avoid many mistakes.

2028. In life we can increase the chances of bigger or smaller successes through the implementation of effective relationships as many and as continuous as possible.

2029. Constructive human relations, effective, harmonious ones help us greatly to achieve a beautiful life.

2030. Unfortunately in the world there are still far fewer constructive relations, effective, harmonious, mutual trust ones, compared to how many there could be.

2031. We should not be a slave to routine again, we must get rid of it and act differently, more effective, more operational, more tactful, more with courage from case to case depending on the situation.

2032. Ideas come fast and we forget them even faster. Ideas come out continuously, without us making any effort. Ideas that we seek, that we want to find we sometimes find them easily, other times very difficult and sometimes we can not fiind anything without looking better.

2033. Our ability to create ideas is a mine which can increase the value and on a continuous basis, without great efforts.

2034. Our ability to create ideas can continuously increase for as long as we live, thus increasing its value on a continuous basis. Our ability to create ideas affects us enormously in our achievement and maintenance of our happiness every day in every situation.

2035. One of the objectives of each personal man is necessary and should be the continuous development as much as the ability to create useful, efficient, positive, humane ideas, which can contribute to the achievement of our personal happiness and maintain it.

2036. As we grow with a grater ability to create positive, effective ideas, necessary to us, the more and more surely we can achieve personal goals and happiness and we can maintain them.

2037.   The ability to produce positive effective ideas, necessary to us is enormously useful and effective as it helps establish, develop, maintain other capacities as well which we can exemplify: 1) the ability to prevent mistakes and failures, 2) the ability to solve problems, 3) our ability to create and maintain happiness; 4) our ability to create, select, set and achieve personal goals; 5) our professional ability, 6) the ability to face any blows of life as big and as painful as they would be; 7) the ability to create and maintain a family, a happy marriage.

2038.   The ability to produce positive effective ideas can increase greatly, easily and with minimum expenditure, with the help of the Internet, knowledge, positive models, which we can find using the Internet.

2039.   Until the creation and development of science and broadcasting them in an easy way for each, which includes the ability to create positive effective ideas, necessary to us, respectively the creation of science, the creativity of each of us, it is necessary to look in the edited books, in the media and on the Internet, whenever existing knowledge is needed.

2040. The Internet can help us in the fastest way, most effectively, the more we find that existing knowledge can help us most achieve personal goals.

2041. The Internet can help us in the fastest way, most effectively, the more we find that existing knowledge can help us most to achieve personal goals.

2042. Sometimes some superstitions may hinder the achievement of effective cooperations.

2043. Reducing the exaggerated consumption of alcohol by as many people as possible has multiple positive effects on the development of the state.

2044. Without dedication we can not maintain an effective cooperation.

2045. In any action we act, we expand its effectiveness if we document everything better.

2046. Effective behaviors help us expand opportunities to achieve positive personal goals.

2047. The solution to be lucky in life is to be perseverant, effective in what we do and to continuously document as fully as we can to know how and what to do to achieve what we want; surely we can have good luck if we adhere to the rules that get us what we want, that is success. I am by your side.

2048. Only effective actions help us achieve efficient co-developments.

2049. Only effective actions help us achieve success.

2050. Responsibility helps us have many more opportunities to become more effective.

2051. The Internet helps us have many more opportunities to achieve effective co operations.

2052. Using more effectively our time greatly increases our chances to achieve more and bigger successes.

2053. Effective thinking helps us achieve performance.

2054. Most world members do very little and ineffective things to prevent the disregard of rights and fundamental freedoms.

2055. All world members need to take all necessary and effective measures to stop immediately and effectively all disregards of rights and fundamental freedoms.

2056. It is necessary and required for states to take effective measures to prevent the formation, maintenance and development of all human vices, because they create enormously negative effects, both for those who have them, and for the others unfortunately.

2057.　Many bankruptcies can be prevented before establishing companies if those who want to establish companies wish to administer them themselves, they must document themselves and learn very well what is necessary to effectively manage a company of the type that they want to establish and administer.

2058.　Everyone is required to support the effects of their own mistakes and not try to do to bear others with them.

2059.　Effective cooperation draws us out from the state of passivity and makes us more efficient.

2060.　Even if we reached a desperate situation we can get rid of it easily mostly because it is written that we live better, not worse, because we have the qualities necessary for this but we should use them effectively.

2061.　Effective cooperation helps us very much to prevent the situation of despair.

2062.　The more effective actions we do are the more chances we have to prevent the situation from reaching despair.

2063. Good morale helps us greatly to achieve effective cooperations.

2064. Psychological balance helps us greatly expand our effectiveness continuously.

2065. Artfulness helps us to discover ruses, but after the discovery they could be extremely harmful depending on the seriousness of the illegal actions made and the size of their negative effects.

2066. The value of an artfulness is zero and can not be compared with a positive gesture as it would have little value, because subtlety has value zero, may not create value, something positive, but only something negative, and it has only negative effects.

2067. The existence of abnormal instead of normality has multiple, diversified, negative short-term and long term effects on all people around the world.

2068. They can prevent many crimes by taking effective measures to prevent crime for each type of crime.

2069. Measures to prevent crime do not only reduce prison terms and large punishments with imprisonment, there are much more effective measures from all points of view including a citizen who spends large amounts of money because of the inefficient legal system based only on prison terms.

2070. Not even in 2007 the majority of states do not apply the most effective measures to prevent crime, unfortunately, but apply only primitive and inefficient methods of punishment through prison.

2071. It is necessary to immediately take the necessary measures to achieve an efficient education suitable to be able to prevent crime very much by this method, which consists in carrying out an effective education appropriate to make people not want to commit crimes.

2072. The state's investment in an effective education that is against the obedience of the law is worth the effort, because if it is very effective with high-quality care it produces positive multiple and diverse effects recuperating the investments plus a large profit if you analyse in terms of financial efficiency the investment.

2073. States should be concerned about citizens especially for an efficient education suitable to all intents and purposes that meet real needs of education of people and society so that both needs are effectively met.

2074. Appropriate effective education that meets human needs and the needs of society is very important both for people and for society, but, unfortunately, even in 2007, many states do not have an effective education that meets the appropriate requirements and education needs of people and society.

2075. We can create a more beautiful life if we are effective in everything we do.

2076. The easier we can produce more ideas the quickly we become more effective.

2077. Confidence in ourselves, in our forces is a quality that helps us contribute and become more effective.

2078. We must create the conditions so that sociable people achieve their objectives as soon as their objectives have positive effects on people.

2079. The more effective our actions are, the more chances we have to meet several favorable occasions.

2080. Correct relations of friendship make us happy and have positive effects on our health.

2081. Life has positive effects on health.

2082. We must make changes only when specifically requested by the actual situation and when they have positive effects greater than the costs and negative effects.

2083. One of the most effective investment companies has an investment in the personal development of employees.

2084. Leaders need more than employees and companies to control their impulses, not to have exaggerated effects in certain situations.

2085. The more we expand more effectively our actions the more opportunities we have that we can meet on several favorable occasions.

2086. The more effective and positive actions we achieve the more records we can make.

2087. True friendship has positive effects on health.

2088. True friendship has more positive effects on friends.

2089. New effective ways of thinking help us vey much to achieve our very special performances.

2090. Effective global co operations contribute to the formation of many true friends.

2091. What is too little and too much has negative effects.

2092.   Countries should promote, encourage and finance more positive and effective initiatives of young people.

2093.   The state's funding of more positive and effective initiatives, useful for the youth and for society would greatly reduce the number of young negative facts.

2094.   Continuously, day by day, it is necessary to have personal objectives, for as long as we live, to effectively manage our time.

2095.   The personal goal of effectively managing our time helps us contribute to the achievement of other of our personal goals.

2096.   Preventive actions help us very much to prevent many negative effects of our actions.

2097.   As we make more actions out of those necessary and required to do, the better chance we have to become more effective.

2098.   The use of computers and information technology as much as possible in making decisions and judgments would lead to the taking of decisions and judicial decisions more accurately, more fairly, more effective and more humane than now taken by judges.

2099.　Without patience there is no effective cooperation.

2100.　Self-control helps us maintain effective co operations.

2101.　Time helps greatly to the achievement of effective co operations.

2102.　Co-development makes us become more effective.

2103.　The Internet helps us very much to expand the effectiveness of our actions.

2104.　As we have more successful friends, the more opportunities we have to take from them effective patterns of behavior.

2105.　Shallow inefficient behaviors must be terminated immediately and replaced with effective behaviors.

2106.　Effective behaviors help us have many more opportunities to meet favorable situations.

2107.　Successes can not be achieved without effective behavior.

2108.　For as long as we live we must seek to have relationships of friendship with special people, who have many successes, many qualities, many positive and effective behaviors in order to learn from them as much as possible. This rule, this principle helps us achieve much easier and more personal goals.

2109. In life we have more opportunities to meet favorable situations if we are friends with as many people who have had successes as possible, people which have qualities, skills, effective behaviors, creative qualities, which are well documented in the areas that concern us as well.

2110. We can make life a lot more beautiful if we only act with an effective positive behavior.

2111. Principles help us be effective.

2112. Compliance with principles helps us achieve an effective cooperation

2113. Only activities as helping others take us towards achieving effective co operations.

2114. Through the Internet, through specialized services the effective prevention of suicides could prevent many suicides.

2115. Corruption in the judiciary area may be reduced by the state very much in a very short time but states will not act effectively to prevent corruption in justice.

2116. Altruism helps us greatly expand the chances to achieve effective co operations.

2117. The more efficient use of our time increases more and more our chances to achieve an effective cooperation.

2118. The more effectively we use our time, the more we can achieve performances.

2119. An effective cooperation helps us get much easier performances.

2120. Discrimination has many negative effects, very high in most states.

2121. Positive principles help us and contribute greatly to maintaining an effective cooperation.

2122. Managing more effectively our time, continuously, day by day, for as long as we live needs to be a personal goal.

2123. Without dedication we can not achieve more effective actions.

2124. In any action we act, we expand our effectiveness if we have effective co operations.

2125. It is permanently a necessary that we have only positive effective actions. Warning. Good luck.

2126. Success is obtained only with positive effective actions.

2127.   Positive effective actions are those that carry out personal objectives.

2128.   Positive effective actions maintain a happy marriage.

2129.   It is necessary for children to learn continuously, day by day, only positive effective actions.

2130.   Each of the parents should be positive and effective models for their children.

2131.   Effective co operations and developments are due to very positive effective actions.

2132.   We can achieve a happy life only through positive effective actions.

2133.   Only effective positive actions should be promoted.

2134.   Superficiality in action prevents us to achieve positive effective actions.

2135.   Bad faith leads to the ending of many effective co operations.

2136.   Effective positive actions contribute greatly to a happy marriage.

2137.   We sympathize those who have positive effective actions.

2138. Sometimes life offers us incredible situations. Some employees are very hardworking, they risk their health and even their life at work for a business to be effective and to succeed and all these employees sometimes steal from the company where they work, harming themselves a lot.

2139. A happy marriage helps us to more effectively develop a harmonious personality.

2140. Constructive ideas help us contribute to becoming effective.

2141. Discovered illegal actions create very large damages often to those who have done them. So, pay much attention, better think it over a hundred times than face the negative effects of an illegal action that you rushed to make. What do you think?

2142. The favorable effects of illegal actions will often be scattered with money for lawyers, for roads and visits to prisons, health degradation in prison, etc..

2143. Thinking long term makes us more effective on the long term.

2144. Being positive helps us become more effective.

2145. We must be happy with the qualities that we have and develop them continuously, day by day, and use them effectively so that we are effective.

2146. Continuously, day by day, for as long as we live we need to more effectively manage our time.

2147. A more effective management of our time, continuously, day by day, for as long as we live helps and contributes greatly to achieving a happy marriage.

2148. Swear words are the effects of debris of primitive times.

2149. Intellectual qualities are also an effect of education.

2150. Intellectual qualities help us achieve effective co operations.

2151. Without dedication we can not achieve effective actions.

2152. Positive ideas help us become more effective in our actions.

2153. Meanness has no positive effect no matter how small.

2154. Envy has no positive effect.

2155. Anger has only negative effects.

2156.   Those who are superficial in what they do not know how to achieve an effective cooperation.

2157.   In any action we act we increase our effectiveness if we have more experience.

2158.   The value of the positive effects of aid given at the time of need is much greater than the aid given in the rest of the time.

2159.   A happy marriage can not exist without positive effective actions.

2160.   Compliance with a promise maintains an effective cooperation.

2161.   Co-development helps us achieve more effective co operations.

2162.   Co-development helps develop the necessary qualities for more effective co operations.

2163.   The Internet is very useful and helps us be able to achieve an effective cooperation with people at long distances. Use it. Good luck.

2164.   Creative behavior helps us achieve more effective co operations.

2165.   Some of the employees of state institutions care only about their person, thus enormously harming the effective and positive activities of the institution for which they work.

2166.   Acting continuously, day by day, in an effective way in order to have success we shall have successes.

2167.   Each parent is required to teach children not to make rash actions, to persuade them of their enormous negative effects, with concrete examples.

2168.   Hastiness in many people has led and leads to enormously many negative effects. Warning do not be hasty again.

2169.   Selfless people must be the imitated in all of their effective positive actions.

2170.   Effective co operations increase the efficiency of those who cooperate.

2171.   Effective co operations increase our chances to meet more favorable circumstances.

2172.   Effective co operations greatly increase our chances to achieve personal goals.

2173.   Effective co operations increase our chances to achieve more successes.

2174.   Mental discomfort present to those who cooperate, created by the relationships between those who cooperate greatly reduces the effectiveness of the cooperation.

2175. The more we increase our capacity to produce more useful ideas the better chances we have to become more effective.

2176. Constructive ideas help us and contribute to achieve effective co operations.

2177. Positive principles contribute and help us achieve effective co operations.

2178. Sometimes, some superstitions in certain situations may destroy effective co operations.

2179. Sometimes, some superstitions in certain situations may destroy effective cooperation.

2180. Without patience many effective co operations would not have existed.

2181. Tact helps us greatly to the achievement of effective co operations.

2182. Co- development makes us become more effective.

2183. The Internet helps us greatly to increase the effectiveness of our actions.

2184. As we have more successful friends the more chances we have to take from them effective patterns of behavior.

2185. Inefficient behaviors should be stopped immediately and replaced with effective behaviors.

2186. Effective behaviors help us have more chances to meet favorable situations.

2187. Success can not be obtained without effective behaviors.

2188. For as long as we live it is better to try to have relations of friendship with special people who have many successes, many qualities, many positive and effective behaviors in order to learn from them as much as we can. This rule, this principle helps us achieve more easily and with greater chances our personal goals.

2189. In life we have many more chances to meet favorable situations if we are friends with as many people as we can who have had successes, who have qualities, skills, effective behaviors, creative qualities, which are well documented in areas that concern us all.

2190. We can make life a lot more beautiful if we only have effective positive behaviors.

2191. Compliance with principles helps us achieve effective co operations.

2192.   Imagination can be developed with low psychical efforts but with potentially great effects.

2193.   Positive imagination helps us a lot to achieve effective friendships.

2194.   Efficient friendships can help us become more effective.

2195.   Efficient friendships can become even more effective.

2196.   Efficient friendships help us create more effective co-developments.

2197.   Inter human effective relationships can be formed, they are not just given.

2198.   Many times abuse causes many negative effects.

2199.   Most abuses can be prevented with the help of an effective law.

2200.   Illegal accusations mostly produce many and great negative effects.

2201.   Illegal accusations can be prevented by effective laws and their correct application.

2202.   Meanness is also the effect of human stupidity.

2203.   Meanness is also the effect of the absence of our home education.

2204.   Greed sometimes has enormously great negative effects for the greedy one.

2205.   Excess in any activity has negative effects.

2206.   Some mistakes can be prevented also through the contribution of the formation, development, maintenance and usage of continuous effective usage of our time behavior.

2207.   Hopes can be created also through the contribution of the formation, development, maintenance and usage of continuous self-effecting behavior.

2208.   Release from our self-imposed restrictions can be made also through the contribution of the formation, development, maintenance and usage of continuous effective usage of our time behavior.

2209.   The obstacles that prevent us from achieving our personal goals can be surpassed also through the contribution of the formation, development, maintenance and usage of continuous effective usage of our time behavior.

2210.   Our resistance to changing for the better can be overcome also through the contribution of the formation, development, maintenance and usage of effective behavior.

2211. Positive experience can be achieved also through the contribution of the formation, development, maintenance and usage of continuous effective usage of our time behavior.

2212. Our resistance to changing for the better can be overcome also through the contribution of the formation, development, maintenance and usage of continuous self-effecting behavior.

2213. The desire to become even more effective helps us achieve more efficient co operations.

2214. Effective daily actions that are completed with passion help us achieve more true friendships.

2215. Our everyday effective actions help us achieve much good luck.

2216. Effective daily actions that are completed with passion help us achieve more favorable situations.

2217. The desire to become even more effective helps us achieve much good luck.

2218. Effective daily actions that are completed with passion help us achieve more personal goals.

2219. The power of continuously being effective helps us achieve more records.

2220. The power of continuously being effective helps us achieve more true friendships.

2221. Our everyday effective actions help us achieve more pleasant surprises.

2222. The power of continuously being effective helps us achieve much good luck.

2223. Our everyday effective actions help us achieve more successes.

2224. Effective daily actions that are completed with passion help us achieve more favorable chances.

2225. Our everyday effective actions help us achieve more efficient co operations.

2226. The desire to become even more effective helps us achieve more personal goals.

2227. Effective daily actions that are completed with passion help us achieve more successes.

2228. The power of continuously being effective helps us achieve more personal goals.

Effort

2229. Some successes are due only to the qualities and exceptional efforts of people without the participation of any favorable circumstances.

2230. The state's investment in an effective education that is against the obedience of the law is worth the effort, because if it is very effective with high-quality care it produces positive multiple and diverse effects recuperating the investments plus a large profit if you analyse in terms of financial efficiency the investment.

2231. A happy marriage remains very difficult but it is worth the effort. Persevere and you will succeed. Good luck.

2232. Although it is very difficult to maintain a happy marriage it is worth making all the necessary efforts. Continue that you will surely succeed. It is necessary to do it and to persevere. Good luck.

2233. There are certain situations for certain persons who do not make excessive efforts and meet favorable situations, which have helped to achieve what they wanted, but they are not at all the same for everyone.

2234. Think of yourselves when you do something legal or illegal even if the guilty one can go to prison. You had better pay extra attention; it does not require great efforts and is not worth doing many years in prisons.

2235.   Achieving a happy marriage is not done by itself, but through many efforts, much dedication, a lot of tolerance, more rational compromises, mutual trust between spouses, a lot of communication, much mutual respect, a lot of knowledge, a lot of wisdom on both sides, much fairness, etc.

2236.   The formation of a happy marriage requires much work, much effort, but it is worth it, though unfortunately they do not do what is necessary, although they have a lot to gain by it.

2237.   There are certain situations for certain persons who, without too great efforts, have met with favorable situations which have helped them get what they wanted, but they are not reachable to everybody.

2238.   Some successes are due only to outstanding efforts and to the people's participation and without any favorable situations.

2239.   Effective state investments in an education that is corresponding and against the disobedience of laws is worth the efforts, because if it is of a good quality, very effective and very attentively created it produces multiple and various effects paying back the positive investments made and an additional huge profit if analyzed in terms of financial efficiency of the investment.

2240. Some of us are extremely glad when we manage to achieve a personal goal or more personal goals, and others have consumed their joys during their efforts in their work done to achieve that goal or those goals.

2241. The successes we obtain motivate us a lot in the efforts to achieve other successes.

2242. Learning and applying strategies of achieving happiness do not require many efforts but many people do almost nothing to learn and apply them although they may help create their own happiness.

2243. A happy marriage is achieved through continuous efforts, through searching, finding and applying the necessary knowledge of achievement.

2244. The necessary efforts and time needed to achieve a happy marriage must be done and allocated because what a happy marriage can offer us we cannot obtain somewhere else and it is priceless for our good and happiness.

2245. The necessary efforts and the time needed to maintain a happy marriage is worth doing and respectively allocating because what a happy marriage can offer us we cannot obtain somewhere else and it is priceless for our good and happiness.

2246.   It is worth every effort necessary to maintain real mature love.

2247.   Imagination can be developed with low psychical efforts but with potentially great effects.

2248.   True friendships are worth the efforts of being achieved.

2249.   The size of our life is made up of several parts of what it is necessary to know very well in order to achieve each of them. It is not easy but not impossible. First we must know very clearly, concretely that we want to achieve each of them, when, how, we want to achieve them, etc.. Among them we mention privacy that includes our family life, human relations with friends, our intimate life, our feelings and our thoughts, our intimate writings, journals, autobiographies, blogs, web pages etc. To succeed in this life it is necessary to respect, know the rules of success in this private life. Then there is employment, which includes ideas, thoughts, actions, objectives and professional projects. And here in employment we can succeed only if we respect the rules needed to succeed in our careers. Good behavior is ideal when we can do that to support our private life as much as possible, employment contributes as much as possible to achieve a harmonious private life, with successful private joys, a lot of satisfactions and happiness. If we propose to realize these needs we will establish that we are able to achive personal objectives and performance, great successes, and we will have joys, happiness and satisfactions in life, both in our private and professional one.

Unfortunately, there are still few people who do what they should not do to have failures in both private and professional lives, or in one of them. The most happy and satisfying are called those who made the necessary efforts and who have managed to achieve harmonious, happy privacy, with joys and satisfactions and who have achieved personal goals and projects in employment. From them we can learn many effective models of action, positive behaviors, which will help us achieve our privacy and professionalism.

2250.   For those who have succeeded in life, who had one or more major successes, the effort they have made to pursue them without problems, to be consumed without having to make big efforts, they made such efforts on their own initiative, without them, someone would do them with great pleasure, without any stress, but it is considered that to succeed it is necessary to make those efforts, those actions. Although efforts, actions were very high, with huge consumption of mental and physical energy, more or less risks they felt of course, normal in order to achieve success, and what they proposed, and this is not to look at the facts not stressed, but on the contrary it has created a state of normality and even additional motivation and desire to do what they have proposed. These ones in contrast with others that the risky, unpredictable, great efforts chased, tried to solve, or attempted to carry out the enormous stress and had much inefficient behavior, but they always made them smarter, more effective, more operational, more powerful, more confident in their forces, in their success, in their future, etc.

Emotional

2251. Emotional intelligence helps us achieve greater results in work.

2252. At times it is necessary to develop emotional intelligence.

2253. He who has an emotional intelligence consists of: 1) the ability to understand others, 2) the ability to help others when needed, with ideas, solutions, and even financial and material ones, a service to resolve the problem, etc.. 3) the ability to see things from the viewpoint of others; 4) the quality and ability to solve problems through relationships that you establish with others; 5) qualities; 6) human qualities; 7) has a good control in any situation; 8) has the ability to easily interact with people; 9) has the capacity and capability to maintain human relationships; 10) has high qualities and abilities to motivate people to mobilize them to work; 11) has the capacity and capability to push people to achieve objectives; 12) has the capacity and capability to keep us optimistic continuously and in any event, and even in very difficult ones; 13) has the ability to never give up under any circumstances even if it appears to others without a way out 14) has high qualities and the ability to trust people; 15) has high qualities and abilities that people have confidence in him, in his qualities; 16) has high qualities and the ability for people to come to the opinion of a request in solving many problems; 17) has high qualities and the ability to gather people around him; 18) has high qualities and the ability to trust himself ; 19) has instinct; 20) is reliable.

2254.　Emotional stability in humans increases their credibility.

2255.   Those who are emotionally balanced have a greater potential to contribute to the achievement of the greater good.

2256.   The man who is emotionally stable has greater chances to meet favorable situations.

2257.   Those who are emotionally balanced have a higher potential and greater chance of achieving more and greater successes.

2258.   An emotionally stable man has greater chances to achieve a happy marriage.

2259.   Those who are emotionally balanced have a higher potential to participate in efficient global co operations.

2260.   A man who is emotionally stable has more chances to achieve a more beautiful life

2261.   Those who are emotionally balanced more easily maintain true friendships.

2262.   Most of the people who have had successes are emotionally stable.

2263.   Emotional stability helps us a lot to achieve our personal goals.

2264.   A stable emotional man has more chances of becoming credible.

2265. An emotionally stable man has more chances of achieving a happy life.

2266. Those who are emotionally balanced have a great potential and chance to succeed.

2267. An emotionally stable man has much more chances to find the right partner for life.

2268. Those who are emotionally balanced have a greater potential and more chances to prevent many mistakes.

2269. An emotionally stable man has much more chances to achieve outstanding performances.

2270. Those who are emotionally balanced have a greater potential to succeed in life.

2271. An emotionally stable man has much more chances of achieving more performances.

2272. Those who are emotionally balanced have a greater potential to achieve their future.

2273. An emotionally stable man has more chances to become even more efficient.

2274. Those who are emotionally balanced have a greater potential to achieve efficient co operations.

2275. An emotionally stable man has more chances to achieve a mature love.

2276. The sense of achievement and quality in everything we do imposes us to use emotional thinking.

Encourage

2277. Luxury should never be encouraged, because it is a waste.

2278. The husband must assess, encourage, respect and reward his wife's positive behaviours.

2279. Employers should be supported, encouraged by states to develop their business, to improve, in order to give adequate salaries.

2280. Countries should promote, encourage and finance more positive and effective initiatives of young people.

2281. Employers should be supported and encouraged by the states to also develop businesses to create new jobs.

2282. We must do everything necessary and required to support and encourage the development of a civil society, of non-profit organizations.

2283. Owners should be supported, encouraged by all to develop their business so as to create new jobs.

2284.   It is necessary and required for the states to support and encourage the development of a civil society, of non-profit organizations.

2285.   States need to support and encourage all those who fight for preventing and stopping discrimination.

2286.   The activity of voluntarism must be encouraged and appreciated at its just value.

2287.   Employers should be supported, encouraged by states to develop a business, to improve it in order to give proper wages.

2288.   Sportive events help maintain health, help develop more qualities and prevent more negative actions, a fact that is necessary to be supported and encouraged.

2289.   States need to encourage, push and reward innovation not be against it.

2290.   Efficient co-developments must be encouraged.

2291.   States need to encourage, stimulate, and reward the more effective use of society's resources both by people and companies for the good of people and society.

2292.   States need to motivate and encourage more the production of ideas.

2293.   The encouragement of positive behaviors is a vital necessity.

2294.   The encouragement of positive thinking is a vital necessity.

2295.   Positive ambition must always be encouraged.

2296.   Oprimistic attitude must be encouraged.

2297.   Optimistic attitude must be encouraged in children when they're very young.

2298.   Hopes must be encouraged.

2299.   Communication between friends must be encouraged.

2300.   True friends encourage each other.

2301.   True friendships must be encouraged.

2302.   Creativity must be encouraged.

2303.   Positive deeds must be encouraged.

2304.   Women must be encouraged continuously to perfect themselves.

2305.   Affectionate   manifestations   must   be encouraged by lovers.

2306.   Affectionate   manifestations   must   be encouraged by spouses.

2307. Lovers must encourage each other to speak about their own emotions.

2308. Spouses must encourage each other to talk about their own emotions.

2309. Spouses must encourage one another's love gestures.

2310. Love gestures must be encouraged.

2311. Lovers must encourage each other's love gestures.

2312. Complements must be encouraged.

2313. Knowing ourselves must be encouraged.

2314. The self-control of our flaws must be encouraged.

2315. Those who succeed to more effectively use their personal time must be encouraged.

2316. The actions of prevention of human errors must be encouraged.

2317. Qualities must be encouraged.

2318. Cherishing oneself must be encouraged.

2319. Responsibility must be encouraged.

2320. Wisdom must be encouraged.

2321.   Will must be encouraged.

2322.   Inter-human communication must be encouraged.

2323.   Mutual trust must be encouraged.

2324.   A great capacity of appreciating people must be encouraged.

2325.   Continuously making ourselves efficient must be encouraged.

2326.   A great capacity of facing one's own life must be encouraged.

Energetic

2327.   A great capacity of having an even more energetic life helps us become more tolerant.

2328.   The self efficient use of our time helps us become energetic.

2329.   A great capacity of having an even more energetic life helps us become more optimistic.

2330.   In order to prevent failures it is necessary to also form, develop, maintain and use energetic behavior.

2331.   We can prevent some failures also through the contribution of the formation, development, maintenance and usage of energetic behavior.

2332.   We can become stronger and we can not allow ourselves to be influenced by the world also through the contribution of the formation, development, maintenance and usage of energetic behavior.

2333.   Creativity helps us become energetic.

2334.   The force of our ideas can be augmented also through the contribution of the formation, development, maintenance and usage of energetic behavior.

2335.   The limits of achievement imposed by ourselves in our mind at a given moment can be overcome or eliminated also through the contribution of the formation, development, maintenance and usage of energetic behavior.

2336.   A great capacity of having an even more energetic life helps us maintain our happiness.

2337.   Continuous self perfection helps us become energetic.

2338.   Will helps us become energetic.

2339.   In order to escape poverty it is necessary to also form, develop, maintain and use energetic behavior.

2340.   Hopes can be created also through the contribution of the formation, development, maintenance and usage of energetic behavior.

2341.   Cherishing oneself helps us become energetic.

2342.   A great capacity of having an even more energetic life helps us maintain our humanity.

2343.   Release from our self-imposed restrictions can be made also through the contribution of the formation, development, maintenance and usage of energetic behavior.

2344.   A great capacity of having an even more energetic life helps us become more pleasant.

2345.   A great capacity of having an even more energetic life helps us maintain our way of being loved.

2346.   In achieving our successes a contribution is also brought by the formation, development, maintenance and usage of energetic behavior.

2347. A great capacity of having an even more energetic life helps us maintain our way of being practical.

2348. A great capacity of having an even more energetic life helps us achieve more efficient co operations.

2349. Our future can be projected and achieved also through the contribution of the formation, development, maintenance and usage of energetic behavior.

2350. The necessary qualities in achieving personal goals can be formed, developed, maintained and used also through the contribution of the formation, development, maintenance and usage of energetic behavior.

2351. A great capacity of having an even more energetic life helps us achieve more favorable chances.

2352. We can overcome the difficulties that we must overcome also through the help of the formation, development, maintenance and usage of energetic behavior.

2353. Communication helps us become energetic.

2354. A great capacity of having an even more energetic life helps us become happier.

2355.   A great capacity of having an even more
         energetic life helps us become more
         efficient.

2356.   A great capacity of having an even more
         energetic life helps us maintain our wisdom.

2357.   Hope helps us become energetic.

2358.   We can contribute to the achievement of our
         greatest accomplishments also through the
         contribution of the formation, development,
         maintenance and usage of energetic
         behavior.

2359.   A great capacity of having an even more
         energetic life helps us become practical.

Energy

2360.   Young people from many countries of the
         world by filling seats that they can in local
         councils, central ones, in the parliament,
         government and other institutions and by
         maximizing the use of the resources
         available (energy, enthusiasm, optimism,
         devotion, capacities, values, skills, abilities,
         knowledge, etc.) can contribute enormously
         much to accelerating the solving of many
         problems of their regims, of their goals, and
         of the world.

2361.   The optimism of the young people is a very high energy of progress, but still insufficiently used.

2362.   Most young people do not use the energy of youth effectively, for themselves, but they waste it in vain.

2363.   Our objectives increase our energy; they give us additional power to attain them.

2364.   Investment in the future also means using to achieve our future objectives, financial, material, human, time resources, our own energy, other people's experience, etc..

2365.   While some are jealous of the achievements of others they could use that time and energy consumed by envy to achieve something than nothing, rather then by consuming unnecessarily time with envy, especially because that time is extremely valuable.

2366.   Where we have failures we should never discourage and lose our wits, our balance inside, our optimism, morale or to start to grieve. If we do this, it would solve absolutely no problem, but on the contrary, it would stress us illogically, abnormally without any positive effects. Those who have achieved many successes knew how to cope with failure, learning from failures, to reduce the negative effects of failures. Many failures rather than strengthening us, they weaken us, they should give us power instead of imobilizing us and mobilize us instead of making them harder to give motivation, instead of multiple negative effects they should have have multiple positive effects.

2367.   However, I disagree and do not consider as logical, positive or constructive the popular saying: „Man learns from mistakes". Man, on the contrary should learn only from his successes and from those who have achieved successes and gained, by imitating those positive behaviors, which have effectively contributed to success. In addition man can learn enormously not to have failures, or make mistakes from the knowledge and positive experience of mankind stored in books, media, on the Internet and the experience of people who have huge experience and knowledge. The more we can prevent more failures, mistakes, the more we can prevent more and more different negative effects.

2368.   It would be necessary and useful the development of a science to prevent human errors because it would prevent a large number of human errors and failures if people study and apply it as much and in as many actions as they can. This knowledge could and should be studied in colleges and universities and other educational forms. In every area of activity for each action type, it could identify factors that create human mistakes and failures and then it could identify solutions and measures to be taken to prevent mistakes and failures.

2369. Efforts and expenses that will be done by creating, developing, learning and applicating the science to prevent human errors will not be much lower than the positive effects of their prevention of a very large number of mistakes and failures and their multiple, diverse and very large negative effects. Financial investment, energy, time, etc.. in these activities related to the prevention of human errors and failures would be very effective and necessary and useful for both countries and for people in particular. Each of us in a greater or lesser way can participate in the creation, development and application of the science to prevent human errors.

2370. Young people are eager for action because they have a lot of energy.

2371. A full of energy and active man must be supported.

2372. People who are full of energy and active have greater chances to maintain a happy marriage.

2373. Laughing plays a part in our consumed energy.

2374. Hopes create our energy.

2375. Positive thinking gives us energy.

2376. Hopes give us energy.

2377. A man who is full of energy and active has more and higher chances to participate in achieving efficient global co operations.

2378. A man who is full of energy and active must be appreciated.

2379. People who are full of energy and active have more and greater chances to achieve more and greater successes.

2380. There are many women and many men who can form and have happy marriages, but they do not find each other although they could. They do too little and spend too little time in finding each other; they consume their time and energy for things that are less important.

2381. Young men have an enormous amount of energy that can contribute greatly with enormous immediate positive effects to solving all local or general problems of mankind.

2382. People who have a high level of energy are very active.

2383. A man full of energy and active must be promoted.

2384. Those who do not have hopes, in order to create hopes for the future need to connect with people who have a high level of energy.

2385. Those who have high objectives in life are mostly full of energy.

2386. The self-control of our flaws helps us a lot to prevent the waste of energy.

Entertainment

2387. Weariness can be prevented through proper diet, education, positive behavior balanced intellectual exercise, perseverance, will, exercise, a value system that we believe in and that we respect, business dynamism, social relations, friends, mature love, a happy marriage, adequate rest when necessary, appropriate sleep, entertainment, etc.

2388. Chronic stress can be prevented through a balanced life, balance, entertainment, successes.

2389. Fatigue can be prevented through the proper nutrition of the person concerned, through education, positive behavior, balanced life, intellectual exercises, perseverance, willpower, exercise, a value system that we believe in and that we respect, business dynamism, social relations, friends, mature love, a happy marriage, adequate rest when necessary, proper sleep, entertainment, etc..

2390.   Entertainment makes us more energetic.

Enthusiasm

2391.   Those who are enthusiastic through their enthusiasm have greater chances to meet more favorable situations.

2392.   Optimism increases our enthusiasm.

2393.   Those who are enthusiastic have high chances to achieve a happy marriage with their enthusiasm.

2394.   Enthusiasm increases and maintains our perseverance.

2395.   An enthusiasm increases our power.

2396.   Optimism maintains our enthusiasm.

2397.   Personal goals also create enthusiasm.

2398.   Those who are enthusiastic become more credible through their enthusiasm.

2399. The state of annoyance reduces our enthusiasm a lot.

2400. The state of restlessness reduces a lot our enthusiasm.

2401. The state of fatigue reduces a lot our enthusiasm.

2402. Optimism creates enthusiasm.

2403. True love increases our enthusiasm.

2404. By orienting towards a future world we increase our enthusiasm.

2405. In order to follow and transform our personal goals into reality, it is necessary to also form, develop, maintain and use our enthusiasm.

2406. A great capacity of anticipating helps us maintain our enthusiasm.

2407. Enthusiasm is very often a force used to accelerate solving many problems.

2408. The enthusiasm of the masses, in some cases, can create some amazing facts.

2409. Sometimes enthusiasm is catching.

2410. Enthusiasm helps us get rid of stress.

2411. Failures should never reduce our enthusiasm again.

2412. A good state of health contributes a lot to maintaining our enthusiasm.

2413. Young people are eager for action because they have much enthusiasm.

2414. Hopes contribute to creating enthusiasm.

2415. Thinking positively contributes to creating enthusiasm.

2416. Enthusiasm helps us achieve performances.

Experience

2417. Human experience accumulated so far, a part of it stored in books, on the Internet, etc.. gives and creates large opportunities for us to have a happy life if we study and depict it.

2418. Successes are also effects of our experience.

2419. The more experienced we are in an activity the more opportunities we have to increase our efficiency.

2420. Those who have a bigger life experience are more likely to achieve more and greater successes.

2421.　Ideas that can change our lives for the better can be found in books, on the Internet, in periodicals and newspapers, from people who have great accomplishments, those with so much experience.

2422.　Our distant future can be changed more or less by what we decide now, primarily for our continuing concern of building a certain future of the great changes taking place in society, of the relations, the contacts that we have with various people, of the information that we come in contact with, of the depth and accuracy of the analysis of information we come in contact with, of the creative capacity of our ideas to create new projects, new objectives in the light of our experience, our present , the information we fiind and receive etc.

2423.　While entering into relationships with other people it is good to take from them as much positive experience and knowledge as we can because they help us achieve the happiness that we all want for ourselves.

2424.　Investment in the future also means using to achieve our future objectives, financial, material, human, time resources, our own energy, other people's experience, etc..

2425.　Our inner potential can be greatly increased on a continuous basis by: 1) the study of more books, 2) by browsing the Internet, 3) by taking, from people who have had great success, their positive experience and ideas etc..

2426. We become wiser through our own reflection and learn from others, from their experience.

2427. Our human experience gained so far, a part of it being stored in books and on the Internet, if we study it and apply it to achieve personal objectives, we will have much greater opportunities to achieve them.

2428. Each of us with the help of the qualities that we have with that of those that we can shape and develop, of the various resources around the world, of the human experience and knowledge acquired in books, on the Internet, in publications, etc. we can be optimistic in our future in achieving a happy future. It is necessary to mobilize the will, qualities given to us with all our being to achieve the personal goal of making a happier future for us. Good luck to all. The ideas exposed by me can help very much, use them.

2429. To increase the number of people who will set as a personal goal the spiritual self-development and who will create greater opportunities for spiritual self-development to be done by as many people as possible who aimed for self-development as a personal goal, it is necessary to continuously create and develop the science of personal development which encompasses the spiritual and scientific personal self-development. Until we create and develop the science of spiritual development it is necessary to develop the science of spiritual self-development because so many people from many countries are more active and effective than the countries in which they live and thus they can be models for other people with positive models of personal self-development and so they can help them create and develop, achieve their personal objectives.

2430. As we have more experience which helps us achieve personal goals all the more confidence we will have in a better future.

2431. The more experience we have, the better chance we have to achieve an optimal morale.

2432. We can have a positive thinking unless we do not have it, through a proper diet, education, intellectual exercises, perseverance, experience, desire, exercise, etc..

2433. An active life helps us accumulate a lot of experience.

2434.   Those who have more experience make fewer mistakes.

2435.   Those who are more experienced are less wrong.

2436.   We can create a more beautiful life if we have more experience.

2437.   As we have more and diversified experience, the more chances we have to meet several favorable occasions.

2438.   Past and present experiences contribute greatly to achieving more and greater successes.

2439.   The richness of our experience helps us and increases our possibilities to become even more efficient.

2440.   Positive human experience is very little recorded in writing, video and audio. It is necessary and imperative that the entire positive human experience be registered and used as much as possible in human activities.

2441.   Experience helps us become more effective.

2442.   Experience and useful knowledge that help us obtain personal objectives give us trust in a better future.

2443.   The level of situations and present technologies, the experience, the education, the resources of all kind allow and impose the development of harmonious global co-development thinking and the achieving of many global programs and projects.

2444.   Positive thinking can be maintained through a proper diet, education, intellectual exercise, perseverance, experience, will, physical exercises, etc.

2445.   The more experience we have to help us achieve our personal goals, the more confidence we have in a better future.

2446.   As we have more experience, the more chances we have to achieve an optimal morale.

2447.   A psychological balance can be maintain once achieved through the proper nutrition of the person concerned, through education, intellectual work, perseverance, experience, willingness, physical exercises, etc.

2448.   Positive thinking can be achieved if you do not have it through the proper nutrition of the person concerned, through education, intellectual work, perseverance, experience, willingness, physical exercises, etc.

2449.   The richness of our experience helps us very much to find our partner for life.

2450. Past and present experiences contribute a lot to achieving efficient co operations

2451. The successes we have obtained have created a special positive experience.

2452. Successes, the stages to achieving successes are very valuable treasures of positive experience.

2453. Through self instruction, through experience and contact with people who have gained successes we get rid of skepticism.

2454. By studying our life experience we can find out where we did wrong, where we did not and we can find efficient ideas which can help us achieve more quickly and easily our personal goals.

2455. By studying our life experience we can find solutions and ideas which help us achieve more and greater successes.

2456. By studying our life experience and using what we need we can become more confident in our future.

2457. Past and present experience contributes a lot to preventing many failures.

2458. The richness of our experience helps us a lot to prevent many mistakes.

2459. Experience often brings us luck.

2460. Young people need and must be very careful not to make the same mistakes as their predecessors by taking from their experience only positive models and experience

2461. Self control can be obtained through experiences, through training, through imitation, through study, etc.

2462. Past and present experiences contribute a lot in achieving a more beautiful life.

2463. The richness of experience helps us a lot to achieve true friendships.

2464. Self-imposed discipline can be obtained through experiences, through practice, through imitating, through learning, etc.

2465. Positive personal objectives are more easily and quickly achieved by those with a greater experience.

2466. Past and present experiences contribute lot to achieving the future.

Biography

Gheorghe Cornel Ardelean was born on March 11.1954 in place Macea, Arad Country Romania Graduate of Economic University, Craiova Romania.

1979-1989 Economist and Chief Economist and sales Department

In 1990-founding member of the first Parliament of Romania after the Revolution of 1989 in PCNU (Provisional Council of National Unity)

1992 - Independent candidate for deputy in the Romanian Parliament, Chamber of Deputies

1992-1996 Advisor to the Arad Country Council as an independent adviser

1992-1996 President of the Commission trade, tourism, services advise Arad Country Council

1990-2002 Director, manager of private companies wholesale

1980 - Philosopher and author books.

1980 He published 118 books, articles in publications, of which 50 English books and 68 books in Romanian

In 2009 - Member and Coordinator of Department programs, projects and activities of the non-profit International Organisation Cornel Gheorghe Ardelean (OIAGC)

As a thought on long-term, positive, constructive, open, creative, humanistic, etc. It has a great ability to create so many positive ideas and solutions, constructive, humanist, creative, helpful people to achieve what they want.

Thinking and ideas sustain and promote the rights of children, women, all people in the world, positive thinking and ideas, constructive, humanistic, tolerante, progressive, understanding and peace between peoples and nations.